Women
ON THE ROW

Revelations From Both Sides Of The Bars

Other books by the author:

Women and the Death Penalty in the United States: 1900–1998

Female Offenders: An Annotated Bibliography (co-author)

Women

ON THE ROW

Revelations From Both Sides Of The Bars

by Kathleen A. O'Shea

**Firebrand
Books**
Ithaca, New York

Book design by Sunset Design
Cover design by Debra Engstrom

Printed in the United States by McNaughton & Gunn

10 9 8 7 6 5 4 3 2 1

Library of Congress Cataloging-in-Publication Data

O'Shea, Kathleen A.
    Women on the row : revelations from both sides of the bars /
    by Kathleen A. O'Shea
      p. cm.
    ISBN 1–56341–125–3 (cloth) —
    ISBN 1–56341–124–5 (pbk. : alk. paper)
    1. Women prisoners—United States—Biography. 2. Death
row inmates—United States—Biography. I. Title.

HV9466 .O743 2000
364.3'74'092273—dc21
[B]
                                            00–039373

Acknowledgments

I would like to thank the community of Innisfree for taking me in almost twenty years ago when I didn't know who I was or where I was going and letting me stay until I found out. Parts of this book were written that first time around, so I am particularly grateful to Lee Walters and the current Innisfree community for making it possible for me to be here again, bringing this work to fruition.

I am especially indebted to Sharon Snyder, Malcolm Richardson, Robert Burrows, Paul McDonough, Matthew Wickerhauser, and Jim Levinson, my Amity family, for putting up with a writer-in-residence for so many months. They offered me invaluable support not only in terms of time and personal sacrifice, but with deep love and understanding. Without their gifts of care and laughter this book would not have been possible.

Two special members of my Innisfree family whose continual support and love make every day a joy to be here are Nancy Chappell and Bill Wiley. Nancy has put innumerable miles on her car running me back and forth to mail things and/or pick up necessities day or night and, in times of need, she has lent me literally everything from her voice to her entire house. To her I owe many many meals and more laughter than one can imagine in a lifetime.

Bill Wiley, a friend of many years, found and supplied me with a desk and chair, a bed, a phone jack, lamps, and all such things that, in his words, "No writer could live without." It was Bill who measured my walls and built bookshelves because "that's what writers are about." And finally it was Bill who cajoled another volunteer to accompany him to pick up my sixteen trunks of books in Charlottesville, bring them to Innisfree, and carry them up to the Amity attic where, he expressed his sincere hope, they'd remain for many years.

To my editor and publisher Nancy Bereano I extend immeasurable gratitude for believing in this project and envisioning a book from the murky and disjointed information I was able to offer in our first few conversations. For many years her commitment to publishing women writers has been an inspiration to me, and it is both an honor and a privilege for me to now publish with Firebrand Books.

Two very dear friends who have been constants in my life and have supported and encouraged my writing in more ways than I can enumerate here are Beverly Fletcher and Suzanne Tewawina. To both of you I extend my steadfast love and heartfelt gratitude.

A warm thanks to Mitchell Karp, an endearing friend, for his "open-door" policy. His initial words of encouragement and love, and his introduction to Nancy Bereano, are the reasons this book was started.

I am particularly grateful to my dear friend Mary Elizabeth Mason for her skillful research in liturgical as well as literary aspects of this book, and for introducing me to the Dream Maker so that I could survive my nightmares and enter my dream world with peace and understanding. Without her gentle presence, I would have most certainly succumbed to despair.

To Hannelore Hahn, Tatiana Stoumen, D.H. Melhem, Susan Baugh, Pat Carr, Dorothy Randall Gray, Ann Loring, Alice Orr, Annie O'Flaherty and all the hundreds of other unnamed members of the International Women's Writing Guild who have loved me into becoming a writer for many many years, I offer recognition and praise. I feel humbled in the presence of the enormity of your gifts and thank you for your continuing dedication to the publication of women's writings in general and of incarcerated women in particular.

Finally, I want to thank the women on death row—Ana Cardona, Donetta Hill, Andrea Jackson, Carolyn King, Virginia Larzelere, Lynda Lyon, Debra Milke, Kelley O'Donnell, Christina Riggs, and Robin Row—for sharing their lives with me. Your many gifts to me, particularly your wisdom, humor, and love, have enriched my life and changed me forever. I can only hope that something of what is written here will make a difference in your lives. I honor you in the only way I know how, through writing your stories.

To Jane Rule,
who told me I was a writer
and that my story would find its place

Contents

And today our Lord answered me, and told me not to be surprised, because just as mortal beings want companionship so that they can talk their sensual pleasures, so the soul—when there is someone who can understand it—wants to communicate its delights and pains, and becomes sad when there is no one like that around.

St. Teresa of Avila, *Cuentas de Consciencia*

Preface

I've been searched, scanned, patted, frisked, and locked in a tiny room alone for about forty-five minutes with an armed guard at the door. It is 1992, and I am at the Mabel Bassett Correctional Center in Oklahoma City, Oklahoma, to interview a woman on death row. I am a graduate student in Human Relations at the University of Oklahoma in Norman. I am allowed to keep a small tape recorder and a bottle of water with me.

People often ask me how I got involved with all of this. And until my book *Women and the Death Penalty in the United States: 1900-1998* was published, my answer was simple: I love research. I couldn't find the information I needed about women on death row, so I decided I would prepare a reference book that I could use that would, hopefully, make it more available to others as well. Even though people asked about me personally, I always thought it was the women on death row they were interested in.

The seeds for that first book were sown when I was a graduate student. After living what might be considered one whole lifetime, I decided to return to school and get a master's degree. I chose the University of Oklahoma because I had an urge to return to my roots. I had been born in Oklahoma City but had not lived in the state since I was thirteen days old.

At first I thought I would get a degree in Spanish. I had spent eight years in South America, was fluent in Spanish, and had taught both English and Spanish for a number of years to high school students. After completing sixteen hours of coursework, however, I woke up one morning and realized that teaching Spanish literature for the rest of my life held little appeal.

That was when I transferred to the Education Department. I signed up for nine hours, met all the white male teachers, attended two classes, and recognized that that wasn't for me either.

My third sweep of available programs led me to the Human Relations Department. I didn't know much about Human Relations as a field, but since I knew I could relate to humans, it seemed a reasonable place to investigate.

Concurrent with my arrival, Dr. Beverly Fletcher, a professor in the department, was engaged in a study of women prisoners in Oklahoma in an effort to determine the causes of the high rate of recidivism. She had organized an interdisciplinary group of professors and students to participate in a multiyear project.

She became my advisor and invited me to join the group just as they were preparing to survey six to eight hundred women prisoners in three Oklahoma prisons. Dr. Fletcher had already met repeatedly with prison authorities to assure that we would be allowed into the prisons to work with the women one-on-one filling out the twenty-three-page questionnaires. For us, as students, this involved leaving the congeniality of a university environment for several days at a time and traveling to dusty, secluded Oklahoma towns, where we spent our nights in cheap motels with roaches and bedbugs and our days in prison cells with incarcerated women. Though every effort was made not to be disruptive, ten or twelve college students coming in daily, sitting with women prisoners on bunks and trunks, on the lawn, at dining room tables—wherever we could find space—was a little out of the ordinary.

Before we actually spent time with the women we had visited the prisons and had met the wardens and guards, most of whom were pleasant enough but none of whom really wanted us there. The project also involved their being interviewed, and some who felt pressured into filling out a survey made our work difficult.

To encourage women to participate we were allowed to set up tables in the middle of the prison dormitories with popcorn, homemade cookies, and punch. This was highly irregular since food generally was not permitted in the dorms, and even those women who did not participate in the interviewing were now free to take food. They stood around and chatted with us while they were eating. We also brought cookies and popcorn for the guards. We had been to several participant observation training sessions, and many of us furiously made notations about what was happening on sheets of paper we had conveniently attached to the clipboards where we carried the surveys. We also drew maps of the rooms we were in, where the cells were located, and noted what kind of privacy the women had.

The guards often tried to intimidate the women who were filling out surveys by standing over them or barking orders at them while they were writing. There were shakedowns (full dorm searches) several times a day with guards sometimes ordering us off the bunk beds we and the women were sitting on so they could tear them apart. We also witnessed pat downs of women and watched women taken away in the middle of interviews for strip searches. We soon realized the show of power was meant for both the women and for us.

The atmosphere in the women's prisons was oppressive, filled with tension and despair. More than one of us would be ill most of the night following a day inside the walls.

It was from the women in the general population at Mabel Bassett that we learned about the five women on death row. They asked us if we would be interviewing any of the death row women, and since we hadn't known they were there, we in turn asked Dr. Fletcher.

That's how I eventually ended up locked in a tiny room in a women's prison in Oklahoma waiting for a condemned woman. At Dr. Fletcher's suggestion, I knew very little about the woman I was to interview, nothing about the specifics of why she was there. Only her name and that she was sentenced to death. Before meeting her I had never thought much about the death penalty, or how and why it is invoked. Since that day I have thought of little else.

I don't know what type of person I expected, but I do know I was not prepared for the woman I met. I was surprised when two guards brought her in and she was about my height, slender with shoulder-length sandy brown hair. She was laden with chains. Her feet were shackled so that she could only walk with a shuffle; her hands were cuffed to a chain around her waist. Sitting knee to knee on chairs facing each other, the two of us filled the small space we had been given. I had already been told that our conversation might be listened to by prison staff, and the four glass walls surrounding us gave me the feeling of being a small fish in a big aquarium.

The thing that really struck me was the woman herself.

She was younger than I and so ordinary looking it would have been very difficult to pick her out of a crowd in any town in America. She greeted me with a smile and immediately began chatting, as if we were old friends and I had just dropped by to exchange Betty Crocker recipes. Instinctively, I felt warm and very next-door-neighborly toward her.

We never discussed her crime, but we did talk about her education, her job experiences, and her family. She had four young children she had left behind and spent a lot of time telling me the things she felt were special about each one of them. Her eyes were tearful as she recounted how the children had been split up to live with various family members, but she quickly recovered her composure to assure me that it was better than having to give them to the state.

It was obvious that she was happy to have someone to talk to. As I listened and watched her face, I began to wonder if there were other women like her on death row, and if there were, why I had never heard about them. I left the prison with a lot of unanswered questions.

After all the data had been collected, Dr. Fletcher let us know that she had a contract for a book, and that any of us who were interested in a particular area could take the data, analyze it, and if we wanted to, write a chapter for her book and be published under our own names. I immediately said I wanted to write a chapter about women on death row.

Since I had very limited data about the women on death row in Oklahoma, Dr. Fletcher suggested I find out about women on death row in other states and do a comparison for my chapter, or, if that didn't work, try a historical overview of women who had been executed or given the death penalty.

Doing the research for that chapter was what piqued my passion for the topic because I realized very quickly that little or no organized information about women on death row existed. As people became aware of my interest, they began sending me newspaper stories, references, journal articles, etc. pertaining to women and the death penalty. I used the Internet quite a bit to contact criminologists, librarians, prisons, and lawyers, and to do research in university libraries throughout the world. Family and friends soon were calling regularly to let me know when there was something about the death penalty on TV. Other people taped segments of shows about women and sent them to me. My personal library of information began to grow.

Several years later, after my chapter had been included in *Female Offenders: A Forgotten Population,* and after I had become a doctoral student, it became clear to me that I needed to organize the considerable information I was amassing on women and the death penalty and write a reference book. The process by which the book evolved included a systematic attempt to contact every woman in the U.S. on death row.

I sent a letter to each of these women for whom I had an address, introducing myself, telling them about my proposed book, and asking for their help. I received responses from only a couple of women, who said that they were not interested and were, in fact, plagued with such requests and just wished that people would leave them alone.

I continued working on my list of addresses, writing to various groups to get information about where the women on death row might be located in their states, calling prisons, picking other people's brains. Then I was inspired to write a second letter, somewhat different from the first. Again I introduced myself, but this time I told the women of my experience interviewing a woman on death row in Oklahoma. I explained that I was writing a historical perspective of women and the death penalty and that their story would be in my book. I gave them the choice of writing their story as they wanted it told or having me construct it from whatever information I could find on my own. I indicated that whichever way they chose was fine with me, but that one way or another their story would be in my book. I also included self-addressed stamped envelopes. This second mailing elicited a larger response, with a handful of women writing back. To those who responded, I proposed visiting them on death row and inquired how I might go about doing that. I thought a face-to-face meeting would give each of us more information about the other. I sent the material I already had collected about them: it was usually returned marked up and scratched out, or with the story as the woman knew it written out. At this point I started supplying a lot of women with stamps and envelopes.

I spent considerable time establishing relationships through correspondence with women on death row, telling them of my life and asking them about theirs before I began visiting them. It seemed that once I got two or three women to understand what I was trying to do, other women contacted me on their own, asking to be included. Then there always seemed to be someone who knew someone. In this way, the circle continued to widen.

As we got to know each other, our correspondence was not usually about their crimes or their cases. Mostly they wrote to me about their families and children, about their lives before "the row," and almost always about how they wanted to help their children grow up to be happy, healthy people. Often they would ask me to send them things to read. This was not information I could use in my book, but how could I say no?

They also sent me photographs, including many of themselves as children. I would sit and look at the innocent, smiling faces and it was difficult to believe that the person in the picture was on death row today. I put the photographs up on my desk and around my computer screen until I had an overflowing gallery of women waiting to be executed. Often, when I felt I couldn't go on with the book because it was just too painful, those child-faces kept me going.

The correspondence multiplied, and my involvement in the lives of the women increased. Looking back, I suppose since the women did not know about each other, each one probably thought she was the only one I was corresponding with. In reality, I soon was receiving a dozen or more letters a week from women on death row throughout the U.S. I was supposed to be writing a book, but I felt incapable of not responding to them. One woman wrote to ask how I had found her; she hadn't heard from anyone on the outside in seven years. Another said she didn't know that anyone knew she was there.

Eventually I told some of the women they could call me. Of course I knew nothing about the arrangements the phone companies have with prisons for jacked-up prices. I did know that prisoners could only call collect and speak for no longer than ten to fifteen minutes. Although at first it seemed like something I could handle, it wasn't very long before I had an astronomical phone bill. I would get four or five calls a week. I didn't have it in me, though, to refuse a call. I was free. They were not. Once a woman called and said, "You are the only one I can ask this favor of, you are the only one I trust." Words like that always make me apprehensive—I couldn't imagine what she was going to ask me. How could I, a doctoral student with no money to speak of and a book deadline staring me in the face, be the only one this woman knew to ask? Her request was even more amazing: she wanted me to take her daughter, who happened to live with her grandparents not far from me, to buy her first bra.

The book took four years to complete. By the time *Women and the Death Penalty* was published, the women I wrote about were people to me. It was no longer a question of whether or not they were guilty. I understood, in fact, that most of the women on death row who are guilty say that they are. They do not try to deny it. More important, as I got to know the women and the circumstances of their incarceration, death row conditions became a human rights issue for me.

Although the book was finished, the women on death row continued to write to me and contact me and send me information about themselves. I knew I could no longer handle the volume of material I was receiving, yet I felt I needed to find a way to let people know about it. That's when I got the idea for a newsletter through which I could inform people about the women on death row and they, in turn, could contact the women themselves.

So I wrote to the women on death row and told them that I was starting a newsletter, that it would be free, and that each of them would receive a copy. I decided to name the newsletter *Women On The Row* because one day I received a card from a woman on death row who wrote: *The women on the row really appreciate everything you are doing for us.* I also told them I would like them to write articles or poems or anything they wanted to for it. There are now 150 subscribers, and I am never at a loss for information each month—only the time to sit down and prepare it. I originally asked people for a donation of ten dollars a year to help with the costs of printing and mailing. In its second year of publication I am raising that to twelve dollars. The women on death row continue to receive it for free, as do many other men and women prisoners. Men in prison have written and sent me money from their commissary funds to help their "sisters on the row."

One of the miracles of the newsletter is that the women on death row became aware of each other. Currently there are eight women who are the only women on death row in their respective states. That means they are totally isolated from everyone and everything except the guards they live with on a daily basis, mostly men. Even in states where there is more than one woman on death row, they are often not allowed to communicate with one another. But after they started receiving the newsletter and reading about each other, some of the women began writing to me as an intermediary. One woman on death row in California, for example, said she could not bear the thought that a woman on death row in a different state could not afford to buy shampoo to wash her hair. So she requested that fifteen dollars from her own commissary money be sent to me to send to the other woman. Women on death row supporting women on death row.

Some prison authorities are clamping down, as they have in Texas, where the newsletter was recently banned for containing "material that any reasonable person would conclude could incite a riot."

If I am praised for my "work" or thanked for my "mission" or sent donations for my "ministry" with women on death row, I am somewhat taken aback. What I "do" with or for these women is what I would want someone to do for me. I write to them, I talk to them when I can, I answer questions they ask if I am able, I tell them about my life, I read to them, pray with them. Nothing extraordinary.

It is essential to me that I talk about what the women on death row do for *me*, which is one of the reasons for the book now in your hands. My association with these women has been a life-altering experience. After my first book was published, I received the following email: THEY GET WHAT THEY DESERVE. MAY THEIR NAMES BE ERASED FROM THE BOOK OF LIFE. I keep that quote in front of me to remind me what the women on death row asked me to say about them to the public. *Say our names,* they told me. These women do not want to be erased from the book of life.

Women On The Row: Revelations From Both Sides Of The Bars is what my encounters and exchanges with women on death row, and some who once were but are no longer on death row, have brought forth for me. It is about how our differences are often less important than the realizations of how we are the same. My life juxtaposed with theirs.

Kathleen A. O'Shea
January 2000

Ten Women

ANA CARDONA

Ana Cardona, a Cuban immigrant from Miami, was the mother of four children when she and her lesbian lover, Olivia Gonzalez, were convicted in 1990 of killing her three-year-old son, Lazaro. His body, beaten with a baseball bat and dumped in the bushes of a Miami Beach neighborhood, remained unidentified for several weeks after it was discovered. The local press ran with the story and dubbed the unknown child "Baby Lollipops" because of the shirt he was wearing. He appeared to be undernourished and had been struck over most of his body, apparently dying from repeated blows to the head.

Ana has always denied abusing her child. She has stated repeatedly that both she and her children were frequently beaten by Olivia, and that she (Ana) did not have the courage or strength either to leave or to protect them. She admits being addicted to cocaine at the time of her son's death, and says she took drugs to escape the horror that was happening in her life.

Ana's lover testified against Ana in exchange for a forty-year sentence for second-degree murder and child abuse. Although Olivia admitted beating Lazaro, she placed the primary blame for the homicide on Ana. Press coverage reinforced this claim, suggesting that Ana was the one who was responsible because she was Lazaro's mother. After her conviction Ana told the judge, "I'm not a monster and I'm not my son's murderer."

Although Ana is the first woman on this list, she is one of

the last women on death row I was able to make contact with. I had written several letters to her but never received any response. This was disappointing to me because I knew from the terrible press she received at the time of her trial that Ana must have a story to tell. The fact that she had been billed as a "lesbian murderer" particularly intrigued me.

I had almost resigned myself to using only the material I had found in other places about Ana when a door opened. Virginia Larzelere, who is also on death row in Florida, wrote to me: *I am trying to teach Ana English*. And that was when it hit me that Ana hadn't answered my letters because she didn't speak English.

Even though I had spent part of my life as a Spanish teacher, writing letters is a different thing. And writing letters that can be understood by someone in Ana's situation was even more of a challenge. In addition, since Ana only went as far as the fourth grade, I frequently had to read her letters aloud in order to understand what she said by sounding out the words. Eventually, however, we established a rhythm and learned to communicate quite well with each other.

Ana agreed to let me write about her side of the story if I would create a consent form in Spanish, which I did, and if I would write her story in Spanish as well as English so that she could read it, which I also did. She told me that she had not understood a word of her trial.

The enormity of Ana's despair is so overwhelming that I sometimes put her letters aside for several days to prepare myself before I read them.

Ana Cardona is on death row in the Broward Correctional Institution in Pembroke Pines, Florida.

DONETTA HILL

Donetta Hill, a black woman, has been on death row in Pennsylvania since 1992.

She was sentenced to death at the age of twenty-three for the murders of two men outside a bar. From the time she was first questioned by the police, through her trial, and up to the present time, she has always maintained her innocence. Donetta believes that her commonwealth trial attorneys did not investigate anything that would have shown she was convicted on false statements, and that her trial was a setup.

Although we had corresponded extensively, it took me a long time to meet Donetta. I had visited the prison where she is incarcerated and met with the other women on death row, but a series of circumstances conspired against our getting together each time I tried. The women I did meet all had their ideas about why no one wanted me to talk to her. One of the main theories concerned the abusive treatment Donetta had received at the hands of prison guards after her death warrant was issued.

On my initial visit to the prison, for example, I was asked by the warden's assistant if I would like to meet with Donetta. Since I had never received a letter from her requesting a meeting (which I subsequently learned she had both written and sent), I was surprised that he brought her name up. But I was certainly interested in contacting as many women as I could and said that I would like to see her. Later, while I was visiting another woman, the assistant came back to tell me I couldn't meet with Donetta that day, even though he had been the one to suggest it in the first place. He politely explained that prison policy would not allow me to meet with more than one woman per visit, and that only one woman could have me on her visiting list at a time. He also told me that making the changeover from one woman's list to another's took approximately three weeks, during which time an inmate's status might change, potentially making her ineligible for any visitors. In other words, he went out of his way to discourage further visits.

Later I learned that on the day all of this happened, Donetta had been told by the same assistant that I had no desire to meet with her and had refused to do so. I immediately wrote to Donetta and explained what had transpired. It was then that we began speaking on the telephone regularly.

Donetta has tried to get the court to allow DNA testing of blood and hair found at the crime scene that did not belong to either victim. According to Donetta, the state refuses to do DNA testing because they prefer not to know the truth. Her trial attorneys did not have any scientific tests conducted, saying both that DNA tests were unnecessary and that the state would not pay for such testing.

Donetta and I have corresponded a great deal about the pros and cons of DNA testing. She had seen several TV shows where experts discussed it, and wanted more information. I've tried to send this to her, including a large research report documenting the cases of several people who had been found innocent and released as a result of DNA evidence.

Donetta feels very strongly that the person who did the killings she is accused of is already in custody, and that the state knows who it is. Her one desire is to prove her innocence so that she can be reunited with her two daughters, who are now being raised by family members.

Donetta Hill is on death row at the State Correctional Institution in Muncy, Pennsylvania.

ANDREA JACKSON

Andrea Hicks Jackson, a black woman, was sentenced to death in 1984 for shooting a Jacksonville, Florida, police officer when he tried to arrest her. She was high on several drugs at the time of the murder, including PCP, cocaine, and alcohol, and had a long history of abuse and domestic violence.

I first got to know Andrea through several of the many people she corresponds with around the world, particularly Audrey Kauffman of Life Lines, an Irish organization.

Andrea had been carrying a gun the night of the shooting because her ex-husband had threatened to kill her. She had gone to his house to pick up her sons, but he had refused to let the boys go with her because she was obviously on drugs. His refusal made her angry, and she left the house and went to her car. When it would not start, she began cursing, then beat and kicked the vehicle until neighbors called the police.

When a police officer arrived at the scene and tried to subdue Andrea and force her into the backseat of his squad car, she shot him. Andrea does not remember the shooting. She testified that she struggled with a "man in black" who she thought was trying to rape her.

During her trial, her attorneys did not indicate that Andrea was a battered woman, nor did they try to find any information from hospital records or neighbors on her history of abuse.

Four years after her conviction, however, when Andrea could speak more lucidly about her past, she was evaluated by a psychiatrist who specialized in using hypnosis to recover memories repressed due to trauma. This evaluation indicated that Andrea suffered from drug and alcohol blackouts, incest and childhood sexual abuse, battered women's, posttraumatic stress, and rape trauma syndromes at the time she committed the crime.

Andrea was found guilty of first-degree murder with two aggravating circumstances: killing in a cold, calculated, and premeditated manner; and killing to avoid arrest. Her case has been in and out of the courts for the past fifteen years, with death sentences handed down on three separate occasions.

Andrea Jackson is on death row at the Broward Correctional Institution in Pembroke Pines, Florida.

Carolyn King, a black woman, and her boyfriend, Bradley Martin, were both given the death penalty in Pennsylvania in November 1994 for robbery and murder. They have also been sentenced to life in prison for kidnapping and murder in Nevada.

I first got to know Carolyn through correspondence, then through phone calls and visiting with her on death row.

Carolyn and her boyfriend began a cross-country crime spree after he was released on a two-hour visitation pass from the Lebanon County Prison in September 1993. Within two days, a seventy-four-year-old retired florist had been murdered. He suffocated after his arms, head, and legs were tied with several layers of clothing, bags, and duct tape. His body was found about a week after his death in the basement of his house.

They took his car, his checkbook, and a credit card and made their way across the country, dumping his car outside Bismarck, North Dakota. There they abducted a fifty-year-old woman from a motel parking lot, forced her into the trunk of her car, drove to Elko, Nevada, and went shopping.

Afterwards they drove into the desert, where Bradley forced the woman to disrobe and lie in a ditch. He then shot her once in the head. Two days later, Carolyn and Bradley were arrested in Yuma, Arizona.

Execution warrants for both Carolyn and Bradley were signed in 1999. Carolyn's execution date was set for May 13, Bradley's for May 11. At one point Carolyn had considered dropping her appeals, but both she and Bradley received stays of execution and are currently appealing their cases.

Carolyn King is on death row at the State Correctional Institution in Muncy, Pennsylvania.

Virginia Larzelere, a white woman, was sentenced to death on May 11, 1993. She was accused of arranging the murder of her husband, an Edgewater, Florida, dentist. According to the court, her motive was the money from his life insurance policies. Virginia has been consistent in maintaining her innocence. Over the years that we have corresponded, Virginia has sent me innumerable papers, articles, letters, and personal documents referring to her case, encouraging me to educate people about what has happened to her.

Virginia's husband, Dr. Norman Larzelere, was shot in the back and killed by a masked gunman through a closed door leading to the waiting room of his office just after he and Virginia had returned from lunch. Virginia tried to stop the intruder as he was leaving. She scraped the assailant's arm and had his skin and blood under several of her broken fingernails, but this material was never analyzed by the police. Nor was the partial tag number she managed to get from the gunman's car investigated.

Both Virginia and her son, Jason, were arrested for her husband's murder. Ultimately, her son was acquitted. Virginia's attorney at the time, Jack Wilkins, made no effort to provide a defense of innocence. Instead, he constantly reassured her that the combination of a lack of evidence and the witnesses' lies would not lead to a conviction. During the course of the trial she learned that her lawyer was "tampering" with the family's money and property. She tried to bring this to the attention of the court and, on her own, filed a *pro se* (representing yourself) motion to dismiss him. The judge denied the motion, however, precisely because it was not signed by counsel and, according to the judge, locating a new counsel would involve a delay and impede justice. Wilkins later pled guilty and was sentenced to fifty-four months in federal prison for criminal activities dating back to 1989.

Virginia was found guilty of murder. Although an eyewitness has since come forward with a deposition confirming the description of the assailant and of the car as Virginia had given it to the police, she is without adequate legal representation and, therefore, is unable to present new evidence in support of her original report to the police.

Virginia Larzelere is on death row at the Broward Correctional Institution in Pembroke Pines, Florida.

LYNDA LYON

Lynda Lyon, a white woman, and her husband, George Sibley, are one of three husband-and-wife teams on death row in the U.S. today. Both Lynda and her husband were convicted of killing an Opelika, Alabama, police officer, Roger Lamar Motley, in a Wal-Mart parking lot on October 4, 1993.

When Lynda first wrote to me it was because she was quite angry about the initial letter I sent out to all of the women on death row. She accused me of not doing my homework and said that any information about her that I had found in newspaper or magazine articles was biased and incomplete. Despite this abrasive first encounter, Lynda was eventually willing to work with me if I agreed to tell her story the way she wanted it told.

Lynda describes herself as a professional writer and publisher. Throughout our years of correspondence, she has periodically sent me one or two handwritten yellow legal pad sheets, titled "The Lyon-Sibley Update," detailing what is going on with their cases.

Lynda and George first got to know each other at a Libertarian Party meeting in Orlando, Florida, in 1991. They married a year later. After an altercation between Lynda, her ex-husband Karl, and George over property ownership, Lynda's ex-husband had the couple arrested for assault.

They fired their attorney at the bond hearing and asked the judge for a continuance so that they could prepare their own defense. The judge refused, telling them that they had to plead *nolo contendere* (no contest), or go to trial that day. A conviction on the charges carried a three-year mandatory prison term. They agreed to the *nolo contendere* plea, and then proceeded to file papers against the judge in the month they had before sentencing, saying he was corrupt and had denied their right to a fair trial. When they learned that the judge intended to send them to prison, they fled with Lynda's son. For three weeks they stayed with friends in Georgia before deciding to head for Mobile, Alabama.

On the day of the shooting, Lynda was using a pay phone in front of a Wal-Mart when Officer Motley approached the car where George and her son were waiting for her. The officer had been requested to check on them by a woman who thought they were homeless.

The disputed events that followed resulted in the shooting death of the police officer, with Lynda arguing that she fired on Officer Motley in self-defense, and to protect her husband, when she saw the officer shooting at him. In two separate trials, both Lynda and George were given the death penalty. Lynda says that she and her husband are wrongfully imprisoned and charged with capital murder because, even though it is unconstitutional, public officials are seen to have more rights and more intrinsic worth than other Americans, and are therefore given preferential treatment.

Lynda Lyon is on death row in the Tutwiler Prison for Women in Wetumpka, Alabama.

Debra Jean Milke, a white woman, was convicted of first-degree murder, conspiracy to commit first-degree murder, kidnapping, and child abuse in the death of her four-year-old son, Christopher, in 1989. At the time of Christopher's death Debra was living with a roommate, James Lynn Styers. She worked at an insurance agency during the day while James, a disabled unemployed veteran, watched both his two-year-old daughter and Christopher. Debra was accused of persuading James and his friend Roger Mark Scott to kill Christopher. She has always denied any knowledge of, or participation in, her son's death.

I first got to know Debra through her mother, Renate Janke, whom I contacted when I was seeking information for my first book. Renate and I corresponded, talked on the telephone, and eventually attended the Conference for the Wrongly Convicted in Chicago together.

Debra testified that she and Styers had a strictly business arrangement for living purposes, and that she neither knew he was undergoing psychiatric treatment nor that he was on heavy medication when she moved in with him.

The day after Christopher was reported missing, Debra was barely able to function and was staying with her family in Florence, Arizona. She did not know that either James or Roger had been questioned by the police. A detective then interrogated her, without anyone else present, and later claimed that he had made notes during their session and written up a "confession." Debra insists she never saw or signed any paper, and was not read her rights. She was given a lie detector test, which confirmed her statements, but the test was not admissible as evidence in court. The Supreme Court of Arizona refused to consider her appeals petition and handed down a warrant for her execution.

Debra Jean Milke is the only woman on death row at the Arizona State Prison in Goodyear, Arizona.

Kelley O'Donnell, a white woman, and her boyfriend/ common-law husband, William Gribble, were both given the death penalty for the murder of a fifty-year-old pizza parlor owner in Philadelphia in 1992. After bludgeoning him to death, they alledgedly took his body to the apartment where Kelley was living at the time and sawed it into pieces, stuffed it in trash bags, and distributed the bags in various public trash containers.

Kelley was the first woman who agreed to be interviewed for my book, writing from death row to tell me she wanted to speak with me.

At the time of their arrest, both Kelley and her boyfriend each individually said that they alone were responsible for the murder. Both were charged with murder, robbery, theft, receiving stolen property, unauthorized use of a vehicle, and arson.

Today Kelley admits being present when William committed the murder, but insists she did not do it. She says she panicked and confessed to the crime partly to protect him. When William received his death sentence, she expected him to tell the court that she was not responsible. He did not.

Kelley O'Donnell is on death row at the State Correctional Institution in Muncy, Pennsylvania.

CHRISTINA RIGGS

Christina Riggs, a white woman, was sentenced to death for the murder of her two children, Justin (age five) and Shelby (age two), in 1997.

She admitted killing her children by giving them lethal doses of drugs which she took from the hospital where she worked as a nurse, and then suffocating them while attempting to also kill herself. Her defense unsuccessfully claimed insanity, arguing that Christina suffers from depression.

When Christina's mother had not heard from her daughter in some time, she called police to go to her home in Sherwood, Arkansas. They found Christina conscious but unresponsive on the bedroom floor, her children's bodies on the bed in the same room. The county coroner estimated that the children had been dead from ten to fourteen hours.

Christina was arrested and charged immediately after she was released from the hospital. It took a jury only fifty-five minutes to find her guilty of two counts of capital murder. They rejected the lesser offense of manslaughter and the mitigating circumstances of insanity. Her execution date was set for August 15, 1998, but she received a stay.

Christina Riggs is the only woman on death row in the women's prison at Newport, Arkansas.

As Women On The Row *goes to press, Christina Riggs is scheduled to be executed by the state of Arkansas on May 2, 2000. Since Christina is a "volunteer," a person who has given up all of the appeals she is allowed and requested execution, her execution date is considered a "true date."*

ROBIN ROW

Robin Row, a white woman, was found guilty of the arson/murder of her husband, Randy, and their two children in Boise, Idaho, in 1992. She was sentenced to death in December 1993.

Robin has corresponded with me longer than any other woman on death row. For about three years I received at least one letter a week from her. She is the only woman on death row in Idaho and the restrictions on her are incredibly intense. It took several months of letters back and forth before I learned all of the rules of correspondence, and every time I made a mistake—such as not including *Unit 4* in the address—Robin would receive a "write-up" for it and I would get my letter returned. The prison said that it was her responsibility to inform me of the rules. If I broke them, even if I didn't know they existed, it was her fault.

Eventually we established a rhythm in our communication that included phone calls as well as letters. Over the years she sent me articles, letters, her own writings, research, pictures, and hundreds of papers to copy. Her correspondence was always mailed in the same kind of envelope, the same writing announcing their arrival. I was so accustomed to receiving mail from her on a weekly basis that I thought nothing about it when one day I casually opened an envelope and pulled out a copy of Robin's death warrant. Her execution was scheduled to take place in only two weeks. My name had been written at the top in Robin's handwriting, as if she had requested a copy be sent to me. This was the first actual death warrant I had ever seen, and I was so overcome as I stood there holding it that my hands began to shake. A letter a week later told me that she did not, at that point, intend to appeal.

According to police records, in the early morning hours a

fire broke out at a duplex apartment in Boise where Randy Row and Robin's two children, Joshua (age ten) and Tabitha (age eight), were living. Because of problems in her marriage, Robin had been staying with a friend. A police investigation uncovered six insurance policies that named Robin as the beneficiary of those who had died.

Robin was convicted and sentenced to death for three first-degree murders that the jury found to be willful, deliberate, and premeditated. In its conclusions, the court further stated that "two additional statutory aggravating circumstances have been proved beyond a reasonable doubt." These were, according to the court, that Robin's anticipation of the insurance proceeds established that the murders were committed for remuneration or the promise of remuneration, and that the nature of the murders established that Robin exhibited utter disregard for human life.

Robin Row is the only woman on death row in the Pocatello Women's Correctional Center in Idaho.

Part 1:

Lauds

A
canonical
hour
of
psalms
of
praise
recited
in
the
morning

1.

I don't ever remember loving Mother and I'm not sure she ever loved me. She did tell me that she loved me many times, but for reasons I've never been able to explain, I never felt it. What I did feel was accepted. I knew they'd gotten me from somewhere, as she often said, and all things being equal they were going to keep me, but my early childhood was basically divided into two kinds of days: the days I pleased Mother and the days I did not. I learned that keeping a balance between the two was the business I would always be about.

As far as the fire goes, it's very difficult for me this time of year. It will be twenty-five years on November 19, and my mother and I were the only two in it. She was twenty-four when she died. No one could get to us. It was in Willowbend, West Virginia. We were visiting friends who had just built a brand new house. It burnt to the ground. I was five years old.

I tried to beat the fire off her and ended up with my face, arms, hands, back, buttocks, and thighs burned. My hair was also burned. Some of my fingers melted together and they almost had to take my arm. There was this contraption for my hand to be in and skin grafts all over my body. I had something like eighty operations. As a child I was embarrassed and humiliated, looking like that—everyone stared at me. Later it became a challenge. My self-esteem was always very low. (Kelley)

Of my siblings my mother would say, "When I had Joe or Frank or Bob or Mike," but of me it was always, "When we got Kathy." She not only changed the verb from *had* to *got,* she also changed the pronoun from *I* to *we.* So although she personally had (and even at an early age I knew that meant *given birth to)* all of my brothers and sisters, I was somehow *acquired* (which seemed to indicate *purchased*) by an un-named *we*.

While I don't recall being officially notified of my adoption, my earliest recollections were that I came from a different place than everyone else in my family. And I knew from reliable information offhandedly supplied by my mother that I had cost thirteen dollars, a sum which I never thought of as particularly remarkable.

The loves of my life are my children. They are the only true loves I'll ever have. I worked hard to make sure they had the best of everything. I have been an exotic dancer, cashier, nurse, nurse's aide, worked at a carnival, and a lot more. I lost all of my family photos and my children's little drawings when my second husband robbed me after I went to prison. So many of those things can never be replaced. It hurt me very deeply. (Carolyn)

Defense worker was typed under the BIRTH MOTHER'S OC-CUPATION heading on my birth certificate. My mother was in residence at the Home of Redeeming Love for three months and seventeen days before I was born. She went, or was sent away, to have me during the dog days of summer in 1944 in Oklahoma City, Oklahoma. Because it was an "in-house" adoption, I grew up knowing, though never discussing, that my older cousin was really my mother.

At sixteen, after seven months of denial, I learned that I was pregnant. I was so afraid, and I did not know what to tell my mom for fear of what she would do. Would she hate me? I cried all the way home from the clinic that day. Scared. I kept hoping that I would just wreck my car and die. Not knowing if my mother would hate me was the worst. (Christina)

In our family, two brothers married two sisters. One of these brother-and-sister couples had a daughter, who would later give birth to me. Since she was not married when I was born and already had one child, the other brother-and-sister couple adopted me. Both were fifty at the time, and why they wanted another child at that point has never been clear. But I remember them as always old. Not old in the way my friends' parents were, but old like grandparents were supposed to be.

I called my sister on her birthday and found out that my grandmother is dying. She needs to have surgery and is fighting that. If she doesn't have surgery, she will die. Her chances are only 30 percent with the surgery. Right now, she is in the hospital. I talked to her last week, the night before she went into the hospital, and I was fine until she started crying and said, "Rob, it's time for you to come home. I need you here." That started me crying. I told her I couldn't come home, that it didn't work that way. She said, "I don't know why they just don't throw the case out of court. Everyone knows you didn't do it." (Robin)

Through adoption, my mother became my cousin, my grandparents became my aunt and uncle, my brothers and sisters became my cousins, my aunt and uncle became my parents, and my cousins became my brothers and sisters. Unaware of any of this, at the age of thirteen days I was taken by train, in the loving arms of my sister, to Salina, Kansas, where I would live for the next thirteen years.

My sons, Shelton, Jr. and Michael, were four and three years old when I was given the death penalty. Now they are teenagers. I have been writing to them for fourteen years.

Despite fourteen years of separation, I have always had a relationship with them. They are loving and respectful to me. My son told me that he comes to me for advice. (Andrea)

As an adult, a younger half-sister told me that the grandmother I grew up knowing as my Aunt Kate had been very proud of me. "I was jealous," my sibling said. "She always showed us pictures of you and what you were doing. I envied you. You were the one she loved." Hearing it for the first time in my forties, I felt cheated to have had someone love me that much and tell everyone except me.

My mother was in a coma and came out of it long enough to tell my grandparents to please take care of me. Later that day she passed away. I'm an only child, but I have stepbrothers and sisters. My grandparents raised me. My grandmother is my lifeline, and if anything happens to her while I'm incarcerated it will no doubt absolutely kill what's left of me. (Kelley)

2.

If the house I grew up in had been a body, the dining room would have been its heart. It was the center of all our activity and the main artery from which the pulse of our family was taken. Yet, in and of itself, it was a small, rather plain room, with unfinished hardwood floors and one whole wall of windows that afforded an enormous amount of sunlight and a view of the Farmers', our next-door neighbors, narrow driveway. It could have been a dull room, routinely sustaining the house's steady beat, except that my mother had filled it to overflowing her precious plants, a cactus collection, and perhaps every picture her grandchildren had ever drawn. It was a room filled with memories that afforded material for endless conversations.

As far as houses or homes I've lived in, I remember living in a lot of houses that were just okay, and then I remember one house that we lived in with no running water or heat, and I keep thinking about how much I was afraid of using the outhouse. We had a bucket we used at night. It was much easier for me than the outhouse. I thought for some reason I would fall in the hole. (Carolyn)

Meals were served on the oval dining room table that could be fitted with extra pieces, should the occasion necessitate. This was the same carved-legged table on which my mother's diaries held court. A clean page for a new day. A new book for each year.

Almost every day someone would come and sit at the table with my mother, and if there seemed to be a lull in the conversation, they'd point to a plant or a stone or something else in the room and she would immediately begin a story.

My family and my childhood have nothing to do with why and how I got here. And this is what people don't understand. God knows that my childhood was something that no child should have, but I can't blame any of the situation I'm in today on that. Understand what I'm trying to say: talking about my family/childhood will not change what I have been going through for six and one-half years. (Donetta)

Men, women, and children dropped by our house in steady streams. Relatives and friends, knowns and unknowns, old and young spilled from our living room into the dining room, through the kitchen and out into the backyard in such numbers that my mother would frequently announce we'd have to have dinner in the park.

There are a lot of gang-affiliated women in here, and I've heard many stories over the years from a few of them. I'd hear them talk a lot about the "west side," and one day I asked where their west side was: it's where we once lived. I remember the days when we lived there and how fun life was as a kid. I feel sorry for the kids who have to live there now and go to school at that school because they will never get to experience the kind of memories I had when I was a kid. I have such vivid, warm memories of those days. (Debra)

A favorite game as kids was playing Mass. Preparations in our living room frequently lasted longer than the Mass itself. Aside from scavenging proper ceremonial attire, there were religious books to be had, a sacrificial altar to be found, holy water and cherry Kool-Aid wine to be made. If the occasion demanded, or on special days like the Feast of the Holy Family, we sent invitations to neighborhood friends to come join us in the making of hosts.

Sometimes we'd get into host-making so intently, we'd forgo the Mass altogether. In which case, faced with the need to dispose of scores of sacred wafers (transformed from Sunbeam white bread), we'd hold an impromptu procession through the neighborhood. On those days, everyone and everything on our block went to Communion. The Connellys' myopic dog. The Gordons' famished cat. The Ericksons, who were Methodists, the Steins, who were Jewish, the Millers, who professed no faith at all, and even the Cantreses, who, it was rumored, were traditional atheists—all communed.

If we ever got to the point of actually celebrating an ecclesiastical ritual, my older brother was always the priest.

My stepbrother, who was seven years older than me, be-
gan molesting me when I was seven or eight, and did so un-
til I was twelve or thirteen. He told me not to tell or I would
get in trouble. I remember thinking it was my fault...I must
have done something to deserve it. But what? I felt so guilty
and ashamed. No one could ever find out. They would hate
me and be mad because it was my fault. So I kept my feel-
ings inside and told no one for years. (Christina)

3.

I moved from mornings of kindergarten stories and games to all-day Catholic school, Sacred Heart, which was two long blocks from home. It was bigger than any place I'd been, had more windows and kids than I'd ever seen. And there were nuns. The first time I saw Sister Natalie I fell in love. From that moment on I never wanted to be anything else.

I had a first-grade teacher who would choose different
children in the class to massage her feet. But the nuns in
school were always mean. I never met a nice one. They
seemed to like hitting you with rulers. (Carolyn)

I liked having my own desk and my own crayons, and I loved the little green box with letters inside that each of us had been given. These prized possessions were safely guarded in a cigar box inside our desks.

We do have a little property, and I sometimes forget
what all they are taking, but I really don't care if they take
everything as long as they don't interfere with my legal
rights to work on this case. To try and save my life and gain

my freedom. Nothing else matters to me. (Donetta)

I still remember sitting at my wooden desk, conscious of my cigar box stored away. Sister Natalie's rule was that when you finished whatever exercise she had assigned, you were allowed to play with your letters. This meant we could make words. I would work feverishly to complete the task at hand just for the thrill of dumping those letters on the smooth, flat surface of my desk. I'd sort them out quickly by syllables and sounds, the beginning of my lifetime love affair with language.

Sometimes I read things and don't understand them too well, or I don't know how to interpret them. I only went to the fourth grade in grammar school. After I was raped when I was ten years old, my mother decided she wasn't going to send me to school anymore. A person who only goes to the fourth grade in school is called illiterate. That's what I am—illiterate. I know how to write, even though I make a lot of spelling mistakes. I've gotten a little better because I have practiced, not because anyone has taught me. I know how to read because I have tried to better myself reading books and newspapers. (Ana)

Uniformity and consistency were the glue that held our family together. I knew unfailingly that on any given morning, as long as it was after 6:00 and before 7:30 A.M., if I opened my father's black lunchbox shaped like a barn I'd find the same basic treasures: two sandwiches wrapped in wax paper, a piece of fruit, some cookies, and if he was lucky, peach cobbler or angel food cake with that white powdered-sugar frosting. A thermos filled with coffee fit neatly in the lid.

I knew, too, that each day while he was inspecting railroad cars, a whistle would blow at exactly noon in the train yard, and my father and the other men like him would gather, find places to sit—outside the roundhouse if it was summer, inside in the winter—and open their very similar lunchboxes to eat their very similar lunches together.

I was five when my stepfather first began touching me, and ten when he put a pillow on my face and raped me. That's when I started drinking—moonshine, beer, and Robitussin. I was snorting crystal meth at eleven or twelve. I stayed away from the house as much as I could playing basketball. It's the only part of my childhood that I like to talk about. I was good, and the boys hated playing against me because they didn't like getting beaten by a girl. (Andrea)

I married Joe Poole in the first grade. He didn't immediately know it, and I only vaguely made the connection when he gave me a red plastic ring from Kresge's gumball machine. Details of the wedding are sketchy, but I do remember thinking it quite a fine ring with a picture of Dick Tracy on it.

My first husband treated me like a princess, like I was the most precious thing in the world to him when I first met him. But then when we got married he changed like you could never imagine. His drinking and drugging got the best of him, and he started abusing me and my son. My second husband also treated me good at first, but he was always jealous or afraid that I would leave him for another man. (Carolyn)

It was Joe who told everyone we were married. It must have been a simple ceremony as weddings go, after which we went our separate ways. I don't think I saw him again for quite a while. When I heard talk about it on the playground, however, the enormity of marriage began to weigh heavily on my mind.

I was accused of stabbing my former husband and then fleeing to Florida to escape sentencing. The truth is that Karl Block received a superficial cut when he angrily grabbed me in an argument. Then he accused us of attacking him so he could, by deceit, take possession of the valuable property we were battling over in court. And we did not flee the false charge: we had already filed papers against the judge, to fight the charge. We left because a friend in the sheriff's department warned us that the judge had ordered a SWAT attack on us in our home, to kill us. (Lynda)

I knew marriage meant having babies, and since I had already decided to give my life to God as a nun, I was not in the mood for this kind of thing. No nuns I knew had babies, nor did I think they would look favorably on it if I tried to bring one with me. Finally, unable to bear the thought of having a child, I threw the ring away.

I was brought to SCI Muncy and taken directly to property, where they went through everything. I had to send my jewelry, including my wedding and engagement rings, my gold chain and crucifix, home. You are allowed to keep your wedding band as long as it doesn't have any stones, and your religious medallion and chain. (Kelley)

As fate would have it, that very day my husband showed up and wanted the ring back. In the way of absentee husbands, he'd traded it even as I wore it for a yo-yo, and was being pressed to pay up. He threatened to expose me and tell everyone I'd lost it. My reputation was at stake.

I saved the situation (though not the marriage) by offering him a quarter, a great deal more than he'd paid for the ring. He accepted, and I became the first woman in our class to marry, divorce, and pay alimony before reaching the second grade.

My husband and I write each other, but I divorced him. It seemed the right thing to do. Actually, I'm engaged to someone else now. There's this guy—I haven't seen him in twelve years—but I knew him on the outside. He's in prison, too, but he maxes out soon. Anyway, he wrote to me in the state hospital during one of the times I tried to commit suicide. He asked me to marry him in a letter and just wouldn't take no for an answer. I've asked him why he wants to marry someone who's going to be executed, but he says I'm not going to be executed, that it's never going to happen. I told him I don't expect him to be faithful to me when he gets out. (Kelley)

4.

Exactly when the God-phone rang, I'm not sure. But by the time I met Sister Lorraine, my sixth-grade teacher, my classmates had been hearing about my plans to enter the convent for years. No one was surprised when I announced my decision to leave.

I do have one constant in my life. By state statute, I am permitted to have a spiritual advisor of my own choosing. Jackie comes in once a week, for one hour of non-contact bible study. The staff even messes with her. They have made her wait up to an hour to see me. She has also been turned away a few times—once because she wore a pair of sandals,

and another time for having a sleeveless blouse on. She was
also turned away when they were too busy to come and get
me. (Robin)

It was with great urgency that I spent much of the sixth grade preparing for my future as a Maryknoll nun. I chose Maryknoll because in a way I felt my family owned stock in the company. My mother had been sending them a dollar a month to save pagan babies for as long as I could remember, and I had figured out from their monthly magazine that they were the nuns who went to other countries in search of these babies. This I knew I could do.

In truth, however, the strongest pull toward this particular community was the idea of impending martyrdom. I was quite sure that if I was sent to some sparsely colonized foreign country, with any kind of luck I'd be martyred quickly and my family would learn about the true extent of my sacrifice in a forthcoming edition of *Maryknoll Magazine*. I knew my mother would be exceptionally proud. If some excruciating torture was part of the ordeal, this was an added bonus.

After I was raped and I arrived home—bruised, beaten, hurting, and half-naked—my mother took me to the hospital where they kept me. I couldn't speak for three weeks. I only cried. Then two weeks after I got out of the hospital I told my mother who had raped me, and you know what she said to me? She said she was sure that I had provoked the attack and slapped me so hard I have never forgotten it. (Ana)

Karen Rivers, my best friend in the sixth grade, decided early on to go to the convent with me. She had never heard of Maryknoll except through me, but this didn't seem to matter. I, of course, was delighted to have a companion on such an arduous journey. The fact that Maryknoll was in

New York and we were in Kansas was of no consequence to either of us at the time.

We didn't take our calling lightly and increased the number of times we met each week for meditation and prayer from two to four. We thought frequent, intense fasting might be a good thing, so we tried it, not just from midnight on, but from when we got out of school until the next day.

I eat once a day in prison. It's all I can stomach. They bring breakfast in at 6:30, always cold. SOS—shit-on-shit we call it—and powdered eggs. I'm a vegetarian, but they won't give me a vegetarian tray. They pretend they do, but it always has meat juices running into the vegetables so that I can't eat it. (Kelley)

Because there were sacrifices to make, we began disposing of our "worldly possessions" with great care. This was something we'd gleaned from a small blue book about another, slightly older girl who had entered the convent. It seemed practical since we knew hitchhiking would not allow us to carry much.

An officer told me that toothbrushes are being pulled next. Apparently, some inmates have made shanks out of them. I guess some kind of finger brush will be given out. After that, TVs and stereos will be taken away from lockdown, too. The other day our tennis shoes were pulled from us. Not from the entire unit, only from lockdown. We weren't told why, but I think it has something to do with two recent suicides where the men hung themselves with shoelaces. (Debra)

We knew nuns prayed and read holy books, and for that we were prepared. We tackled the lives of several saints, amongst whom St. Bernadette of Lourdes was a favorite. She was the closest to our age, and there was a movie about her life. Another favorite was Therese of Lisieux, who washed the bodies of lepers and then drank the water she'd washed them in to show they did not revolt her in any way. This type of sainthood didn't really appeal to me, but I was awed by these courageous lives and baffled by the mixed feelings they aroused.

We are only permitted three showers in a seven-day period. We are young women with female issues that men do not have. When a woman is on her menstrual cycle, daily hygiene is the most important thing. Three pairs of underpants may be fine for men, but women have hygienic problems which we have no control over. We should be allowed a change of underwear every day. (Carolyn)

As our time to leave grew closer, we became nervous and excited about the supreme sacrifice we were poised to make. With only one week left before our impending departure, Sister Lorraine, as if she somehow knew, put pamphlets about Maryknoll on a small table in the back of the classroom. Karen and I scooped them up immediately, not at all sure she hadn't intended them for us in the first place.

It was only then that we had any clue you couldn't just show up at the doors of the Maryknoll convent uninvited— even if it was God who had called. There were forms to be filled out and, in one place, it actually informed us that we had to apply. Our spirits hit rock bottom when we read: ALL APPLICANTS MUST BE TWENTY-ONE YEARS OF AGE.

There wasn't any need to read further. We resigned ourselves to finishing the sixth grade with our classmates.

Yes, we are here together on death row, but our hearts

and minds are set on very different goals. What the others do here is their business. But when their business affects me in any way, the best thing I can do is back off. (Andrea)

I recuperated from the setback reluctantly and gave up my religious calling for Raymond. He was what I needed to ease the pain. We'd been in the same class since the first grade, but it wasn't until the seventh that he seemed interesting.

In grade school, around the age of twelve or thirteen, I started to develop. All of the boys noticed me and I became a cheerleader and I had lots of boyfriends. I really started believing what other people were telling me—that I was beautiful and smart (because I made good grades), and it was wonderful. (Carolyn)

It wasn't that Raymond and I really cared about each other. It was just that Sister Bridget was incensed by the thought that we did. I even replaced my miraculous medal with Raymond's arrowhead ring.

At age fourteen we moved, and I began drinking, smoking pot and cigarettes, and sneaking out. I was making friends, but I still felt alone and different. I felt that no boy liked me because of my weight, so I became sexually promiscuous because I thought that was the only way I could get a boyfriend. I was so desperate to be loved that I couldn't see that what I thought was being cared about or loved was just sex for them. I began to believe that was all that I deserved, no matter how much I wanted it to be more. The sad part was that I never enjoyed the sex—I did it to please them and to feel loved. (Christina)

5.

The promise of a religious life returned once again the day a group of girls in blue uniforms filed into our classroom in the eighth grade and stood facing us in a long straight line.

Sister Cortona Marie introduced them as *aspirants*. They were high school girls studying to be nuns and they actually lived in a convent. After the trauma of the sixth grade, I was amazed to learn that convents accepted high school students. I sat there mesmerized, as if a band of angels had suddenly appeared and were calling me by name.

*They took me to Starke to be executed five days early for security reasons. I had this motorcade, with two armed officers inside with me and two cars in front of me. They were really mad when they had to turn that death caravan around and bring me all the way back. Coming down, they were laughing and joking. They said I'd fit just right in the chair. I was riding with this one officer, who was angry about my stay of execution. Turning around she said to me, "You can be sure, it might not be today, and it might not be tomorrow, but one of these days we're gonna fry your black ass."
(Andrea)*

A few weeks later, I joined other interested girls in a day trip to the Nazareth motherhouse of the Sisters of St. Joseph, sixty miles away in Concordia, Kansas.

It was everything I had hoped for. I saw more nuns congregated in one place than I'd seen before, and the girls who had visited our classroom were there, too. They seemed to glow. They spoke in soft tones and showed us around with evident pride.

Starting September 23, we will only be allowed a single one to two-hour visit per month. I have no immediate fami-

ly that live in this state. All of my visitors drive from Virginia, Maryland, Oklahoma, and California for a one-hour visit. I will be denied visits because my family cannot afford to drive or fly all of that distance for one hour. It is already devastating enough that I cannot touch or hold my children. Why must I be denied permission to see them altogether? (Carolyn)

I decided not to go to Sacred Heart High School the following year, but to attend the Apostolic School (the official name) instead. It was then my mother told me I might not be accepted if I applied. According to her, the church didn't want or accept illegitimate children as candidates for religious life.

At first I felt angry that the circumstances of my birth might have something to do with whether or not I was worthy of becoming a nun. But then we learned that for church purposes I had been legitimized by my adoption. I applied and was accepted without problems for the following September.

When I was twelve I wanted to be a nun, but my mother reminded me that I was impure because I had been raped, and to be a nun you had to be pure. (Ana)

My family drove me to the motherhouse. As a veteran of one visit, I knew the way. In the parking lot behind the main house we found a number of other cars with parents, nuns, relatives, and friends of girls who, just like myself, were coming to stay. People were emptying cars and carrying boxes and other possessions through the back door.

That afternoon, as we all gathered in the auditorium, I had the exhilarating feeling of belonging to something truly amazing. It may have had a lot to do with the uniform, or because we were fifty-four strong, healthy high school girls who had left our homes to give our lives to God. I really don't know. But I, for one, was happy that God had called.

When I first got here in 1984 they didn't have a place for death row women cause there weren't any. So they made a special room and locked me in there. There was this screen in front of my door, and one day one of the girls helped me dig out a corner, helped me pull it out, so that she could sneak me cigarettes and matches. I was a smoker then. And sometimes the other girls would come over and talk. Later they built us a place of our own and I was moved there. There's not a lot to see. (Andrea)

I was introduced at the Apostolic School to the different groups of women living there—aspirants, postulants, novices, junior professed, and professed sisters. There was also the Superior General, who sounded very important to me.

In my five years on death row I have seen the superintendent [warden] three times, two of which she was accompanied by the commissioner of corrections. The superintendent is supposed to be impartial and not try to punish us more through terrible living conditions, surroundings, or by subjecting us to the verbal and physical abuse of unprofessional officers. (Kelley)

I also learned about silence. We were instructed never to talk to the sisters unless specifically told to do so. That there were certain places in the convent where we were not permitted to talk at all. When it got right down to it, in fact, there were very few places where we could talk. It was made clear that if we had anything to say to anyone, at any time, anywhere, we should whisper.

I don't come out of my cell or talk to people for weeks. I've gotten used to being locked inside and mostly like to keep to myself. I can talk to the other girls when they take us out into the yard, but being alone has been my life for fourteen years now. I guess I've become institutionalized. I get along with me. I guess that what I'm saying is, over the years, you adjust. (Andrea)

By and large I loved the Apostolic School and what it meant, as much as I could at that age. It was a place where I shared my hopes and dreams of being a nun with girls who had similar hopes and dreams. The year at Nazareth gave me a feel for the religious life. A taste of the real thing. We walked and talked, laughed and sang, warmed each other's souls and loved each other's hearts. We prayed and learned discipline. There were many tears and much laughter. It was a time of planting seeds to be harvested in other seasons.

At the end of the year my parents were told that I needed to stay home until I was "more mature." My mother never got over it. I returned to my parents' house filled with even greater determination to "grow up" and become a nun.

At age thirteen I was molested by a neighbor's husband, and in trying to deal with those feelings, with low self-esteem and no sense of belonging, I began drinking. One night, while I was drunk, I had my first sexual encounter [consensual] with someone I knew only by his first name. When I realized what I had done, I cried. I was scared and alone and I didn't know what to do. My cousin found me sitting on her tailgate crying. I didn't want to tell her, but with me crying, it didn't take long for her to figure it out. So I told her, and her boyfriend eventually beat the guy up. I was not only embarrassed but also ashamed of what I had done, and I was afraid of what my cousin thought of me. This became another secret. I couldn't tell, not only for myself, but also for her because we were not supposed to be there and she would have gotten in trouble. (Christina)

6.

The book that changed my life forever fell off the shelf one afternoon during my junior year while I was hanging out, as I often did, in the library. I picked it up and, at first, just stood there and stared. As books go, it wasn't all that attractive. It was a paperback, regular size, maybe a blue cover. *The National Guide to Catholic Sisterhoods* was emblazoned across the front. When I turned it over it opened, and I found myself face-to-face with a nun from a community where, I can't say how as they were strangers to me then, I was sure I was supposed to be.

Because of my experience with the Maryknoll order in the sixth grade, I immediately looked at the requirements. They included: "Girls may be received as postulants who have completed their fifteenth year. Normal mentality and a doctor's health certificate are required."

I am still not eating and when I do I purge. I know it's a slow way to die, but I am in a pattern now and I can't seem to stop it. My attorneys are trying to get me help, but I don't know. I just feel like maybe this is the way it was meant for it to end for me.

I have been sick for over three weeks. I had pneumonia and I felt so weak I couldn't do anything. I have been having a really hard time. I have been having those crazy thoughts again and I don't feel like going on at all anymore. How I make it through each day is beyond me. Because I feel like I have nothing to live for and I don't know. (Carolyn)

I left the library that day as close to what I imagined heaven to be as I could remember. There was a sweet, strong smell of fresh-cut alfalfa in the air as I rushed home to tell my mother I wouldn't be going to Sacred Heart for my senior year in high school.

Her first question after I said I was going to enter another community was, "Where are they?"

I responded, "New York."

She said, "Go tell your father."

My father was reading the *Salina Journal* when I broke the news to him. He stopped long enough to fold back one of the pages, look up at me, and ask, "Are you sure this is what you really want?"

"Yes," I told him.

"Well," he said, "just remember it's a long walk home."

I wrote a letter of inquiry to the address in the book and received an answer with an envelope full of information. I learned that although the motherhouse was in White Plains, New York, the aspirancy was in Peapack, New Jersey. Those details seemed unimportant to me, as I was on a quest for God. Limits of space and time simply didn't count.

Our fight has now become psychological warfare. Hooper [Alabama Supreme Court Justice] has directed the bottom-feeding prison psychiatrist to trick us into revealing exploitable weaknesses. He sent a sleazy lawyer here to try to coerce me into accepting his "help." He has spies and agents inside the prisons to send him copies of the letters George and I send to each other. But we press on. Despite this newest development, we are going on to Congress. (Lynda)

Toward the end of August 1961, my parents withdrew their four hundred dollars in savings from the Farmers State

Bank, and we set out across the plains. We were tightly packed in the blue family Studebaker headed for St. Joseph's Villa in Peapack, New Jersey. I had applied to be an aspirant and had been immediately accepted. We drove for days, finally reaching the country lane where the villa was located. The road wound into a long, tree-lined driveway and ended at a towering wrought-iron gate.

I've already taken that ride, handcuffed and shackled in the back of a van, to the electric chair housed in the men's prison in Starke, 342 miles away from the women's prison. We were on the highway when a stay of execution was issued. The motorcade was flagged down, and they were told to turn back. I could see how disappointed some of the officers were. They came back to the van with long faces. (Andrea)

When we arrived, no one said a word. My father stopped the car, which suddenly looked out of place, and my mother told me to get out and go to the door and present myself. She said they'd wait there.

The front doors were enormous, and I felt small and somewhat anxious as I rang the bell. An elderly nun appeared. All I could do was mumble my name. I was relieved to see she wasn't surprised and, in fact, smiled and seemed rather pleased. She motioned me into a large parlor without saying much and pointed to a chair for me to sit in. Then she left me alone for quite a while. I sat there nervous and pensive, completely engulfed by the enormous space.

The "hole" originated many many years ago. In the old days, inmates sent to solitary confinement were put in a hole. I live in the hole. Always have. Pocatello Women's Correctional Center doesn't have a section for death row. So I am here, but separated from the ones in solitary confinement or isolation. I can hear them if they yell to each other, but I cannot communicate in any way, shape, or form. (Robin)

St. Joseph's Villa, located on a beautiful estate in New Jersey's Somerset Hills, had been purchased by the community as a retreat house. In the early mornings, if you crossed the outdoor walkway that connected the aspirancy to the main house, you'd find yourself above the clouds looking down into mist-covered valleys on either side. This did much to add to the surreal effect of it all.

When I look out my window, my view is a large parking lot with the foothills in the distance. The window is sealed. When I look out my window in my door, I see the day room that I pass through to go to the shower or to use the telephone. I also see part of another enclosed tier (as mine is) that houses closed-custody women and part of the office to my unit. (Robin)

I'd only seen rooms like this in movies. The ceilings were extremely high, the antique furniture massive. Heavy green and gold curtains hung from the windows. It felt a little like a museum. I had a strong urge to open the curtains. Instead, I thought of my family out in the car and wished they had come inside with me.

I was placed in a cell that had paint peeling off the walls and floors, feces stains, bloodstains, filth. It was so dirty I could not clean the walls, and the windows were so black you could not see out. When you flushed the toilets, feces, urine, and tissue came up in the neighbor's cell and vice versa. There was absolutely no proper ventilation or heating. The windows were not insulated or caulked, so that the winter wind would just blow in. We were only allowed two blankets. (Carolyn)

I was never officially told I'd entered an Italian community. After a while, it just became obvious. The aspirants were mostly second-generation Italians; they spoke English and at least understood Italian. The sisters who were responsible for running the house, however, were from Italy, and Italian was their native language.

The first few nights I cried myself to sleep. I wanted to go home. I didn't understand most of the things that were said to me, and although I liked my new friends, it seemed as if the nuns were always shouting.

The mentally ill or behavior problem inmates would kick and bang on the doors, scream at the top of their lungs for hours, smear feces all over the room that we had to smell, throw urine through the door or wicker, flood the rooms and hallways, and kick cinderblocks out of walls. That's why they made a steel room—everything is steel, including the walls. (Carolyn)

We prayed and ate largely in Italian. I didn't like going to chapel because the prayers were in a language foreign to me. Even saying the rosary seemed unbearably long. Meals were a trial: in spite of eating in silence, there was grace to intone in Italian. Then someone read lengthy passages from books, which were rendered totally meaningless to me by the language barrier. At least three times a week we had dishes whose names I couldn't even pronounce. As the days wore on, I had a sinking feeling I'd never see fried chicken or peach cobbler again.

I am still trying to stay strong, but a lot has been going on with me and I have stopped eating any of the food that they give us here. So I try to buy the protein bars and instant breakfast from the commissary and non-fat milk. But that's becoming hard because my family is unable to help me right now with money. Food comes cold in a styrofoam container with hair in it most of the time. (Carolyn)

I didn't have the nerve to ask my parents to take me home in those first few days. They'd sacrificed so much to get me there, and my father's question—*Are you sure this is what you really want?*—weighed heavily on my mind.

When I pulled myself together, I decided I'd give it a try. What did I have to lose? I was a senior in high school and, if nothing else, it would be an adventure. I could leave after graduation. I could go home to the sisters I already knew. I was certain I'd be mature by then, and they would want me back.

I went through a five-week trial, February 1–March 5. Half the time I was there physically but not mentally, and when I was there I was a basket case. I sat there while the prosecutor took sentences or incidents and twisted and turned them, until even I thought I was guilty. I found out that all a trial was were two stories being told and the jury believing the better story. The story my jury liked the most was the prosecutors'. They found me guilty on all counts. Then I was escorted back to county jail where I had been for over a year. I learned firsthand that our justice system needs some serious changes, but it won't change in my lifetime. Police, prosecutors, lawyers, and judges are all people, and they lie just as other people do. (Robin)

We attended regular high school classes at Mount St. John Academy in Gladstone, a boarding school owned and operated by the community. It was my first experience with privileged families who send their children away to school. The fifteen of us commuted daily in a large sixteen-passenger limousine to our classes. On a good day, it was about a twenty-minute drive down one mountain and up the other. In the winter, it took longer, and sometimes we didn't make it at all.

Once we were moved to the death row unit we were told that we would have a law library for us—the death row inmates. Then the next word was we would not be getting a law library here in the unit for us to use, but instead we could write to the librarian and request whatever cases and information we needed. I have tried this, and 95 percent of the time she writes back and says she can't give me any cases until she has the case numbers. It is impossible for us to get these numbers since we don't have any legal books or materials to look them up in. So what are we supposed to do? (Carolyn)

It was the middle of the year when the Cubans arrived. We were told they'd escaped from Communism and that they didn't speak English. Many Cuban children were being placed in Catholic boarding schools throughout the U.S. They had been sent out of their country alone and needed places to live. About twenty came to Mount St. John.

When I came to this country I was nineteen. I didn't want to come because I didn't know anyone here and, at the same time, I didn't want to stay in Cuba because I hated the Communists. The situation in Cuba was horrible. But my mother convinced me to leave, promising she would join me later. This never happened. (Ana)

Somehow Sister Thomasina, the Mistress of Aspirants, got the idea I could teach these new arrivals English. I didn't speak Spanish, and I didn't have a clue about how to instruct someone else in speaking English, but she said it'd be no problem for me and offered my services to the school. I became an English teacher one sunny afternoon in the boarders all-purpose room at Mount St. John Academy in my senior year in high school. I've been one, in one form or another, ever since.

I pointed to everything. Point and name, point and name. They would repeat whatever I said, and I would beam with pride each time they struggled to say a word. They went out of their way to please me, opening a whole new world for me. I was as excited as they were by their learning.

I feel bad because I don't know what to do. I see that other women here get law books from the library and look up the laws about their cases and confront their attorneys if they are telling them something wrong. But since I don't speak English, I don't understand anything about these books, and even if I did, they are only in English. I can only hope for justice. (Ana)

My postulant year rushed to a close. I graduated, returned to Kansas for three months at home with my family, then flew back to New York to enter the novitiate. As the plane approached Kennedy airport, it dipped low over the enormous adjacent cemetery, seemingly in reverence to the thousands buried there. My life was just beginning.

7.

Memories of midwestern wheat fields and long summer sunsets faded as we pulled out of the airport that day. I wasn't interested in conversation. My mind was racing far beyond the traffic on the Long Island Expressway. I had reached a milestone in my life, and nothing could override the impact: I was entering the novitiate as a postulant. I was becoming a nun. I would wear a religious habit and be called sister-mary-something. I had given my life to God.

I don't keep a journal. Reason? They could read it if it's in my room. They can read my letters, too, even though they have already gone through the mailroom. I feel it's none of their business. I have a contact officer, who I should talk to each week. She gets really frustrated with me. I'm to talk to her with my problems, etc., and I won't. Everything I tell her is written in my file for all to see. If I was to say something negative I know there would be repercussions. They say there won't be, but it happens all the time. So, I say, "I'm fine," even when it's obvious that I'm not. (Robin)

Beyond the town of Glen Cove huge estates dotted the expansive landscape like occasional seeds in a luscious melon. Names like Colgate, Vanderbilt, DuPont, and Firestone were our most formidable neighbors. Immaculate Heart Novitiate had formerly been the 250-acre 56-room summer home of financier J.P. Morgan, set amidst luxurious gardens, a spacious open field, and a private beach.

This building couldn't possibly legally pass inspection. It should be under investigation. The Restricted Housing Unit is located on the outside of the prison compound about one-half mile away in what looks like a condemned building. I was put in a filthy cell. They denied me any cleaning supplies and told me to use a sanitary napkin to do my floor. My socks were black from the filth in the cell. The mattress had blood and urine stains all over it. The sink and toilet were filthy. All of the linen, towels, and washcloths had stains on them. (Kelley)

The term *novitiate* can be confusing, because although it referred to the building where we were housed, it also referred to what we were doing there. If a young woman wanted to be a nun, she entered a novitiate, a religious boot camp of sorts.

Three very different but intricately related groups made up the novitiate. The first and most visible was the professed sisters. They were the "lifers," nuns who had lived in the community for several years and had made a decision mutually with the community to stay. They were what each postulant and novice hoped to become.

The only difference between our sentence and a lifer's is we die by unnatural causes and they die by natural ones. (Carolyn)

The second group was the novices. You could become a novice and wear a habit with a white veil after a year as a postulant—if Mother Mistress, the nun principally responsible for your religious training, and the community thought you were ready. If they didn't, you were either sent home or given an extended postulancy. This was something like being left back a grade in school: you would be in the same building with all your friends, but they would be a grade ahead.

As postulants, the third group, we were not allowed to speak to the professed sisters. We knew, however, that they were there, and that their very presence was important to our religious formation. This knowledge was an enduring bond between us. They took care of the basic essentials of running the house. They cooked our meals, sewed our clothes, and planted the gardens we enjoyed. They shopped, made doctors' appointments, and picked up travelers at the nearby airport. They were responsible for all our contacts with the outside world. Because of them, our lives in the novitiate remained quiet and secluded.

They've tried to assassinate me twice but failed. They placed spies in prison to copy our letters and report our reactions to their various harassments. And I am again delayed in completing and sending the petition due to a deliberate and methodical program of harassment and persecution against me by certain officers and administrators of this prison and the Department of Corrections in Alabama.

The harassments include sleep deprivation, threats of punishment for imagined or minor violations of vague prison rules, and the denial of privileges normally given death row prisoners here. This has caused me debilitating migraine headaches, stomach problems—such as nausea and an inability to eat more than a few bites of food at a time—as well as extreme exhaustion and mental lethargy. (Lynda)

Although novices and postulants had separate daily schedules and were forbidden to talk to one another, we all lived in the same space and used the same rooms.

The four of us can talk when we go out to the walkyard. This is for one hour, four days a week. It depends on the guard who is on if we can talk back and forth from one cell to the other. I've heard that in other prisons the women on death row are treated differently, that some can work. It is terrible to be in one cell for so many hours. (Ana)

The postulancy was a time of testing—a "gentle testing," I read somewhere. But the thing that has stayed in my mind is the cleaning we did. Few of us were experienced housekeepers when we entered, although those of us who had been aspirants had better preparation than most. Everyone knew the basics, but even Peapack was no match for the endless possibilities of the Morgan mansion. In some ways cleaning every day was discouraging since nothing ever had a chance to get really dirty.

If you can imagine a massive cleaning machine made up of forty or so healthy young women, and some twenty slightly older but just as healthy women, in motion constantly. If you can further imagine that when these individuals weren't cleaning they were praying rather than messing things up, you might have a clue what things were like. The truth is that the novitiate was always spotless. If, on rare occasions, we found a dust ball, it was cause for great joy.

As far as cleaning the RHU hallways, steps, and showers, they are occasionally done by general population details who do not sweep, but mop with a black filthy dirty mop head. They do not change shower curtains or scrub the showers. The only time the RHU is cleaned well is if inspection by the state or board of health is scheduled, or the commissioner is coming. When an inmate leaves the RHU the cell is not cleaned or swept or mopped by anyone, but immediately filled with another body. (Kelley)

Reenforcing my aspirant training, the most significant lesson we learned as postulants was silence, Sacred Silence being the most serious. This period began officially each evening after community recreation when we'd line up, one by one, and kiss the large silver crucifix Mother Angelica wore suspended on her breast. As we bent down, we'd say, "Goodnight, Mother," and accuse ourselves of any minor infractions of the holy rule that had taken place that day.

They do conduct reports every thirty days for things like cleanliness, use of time, whatever. On one of the reports they said my cleanliness was unsatisfactory. That offended me. Another report said that I questioned everything. Well, why can't I? (Kelley)

Religious decorum was something we heard about all the time. We were told to "maintain" religious decorum, and maintaining it presumed we already had it, I thought. But only after many laborious hours of careful training, in everything from how to pick up a fork to how to eat corn on the cob, did we learn to walk, talk, think, eat, and sleep in a way our community defined as religious.

When I got my own homes they were always showcase homes. Everything was in order. I even had a maid to clean because I worked so much and after work I did things with my children. But I always had to have things run the way that I said and the children had things that they had to do in the house, especially like taking care of their own rooms. And there was no reason for their homework not to be done by dinnertime and ready for me to check. (Carolyn)

Part of religious decorum involved custody of the senses. The novitiate was the major training ground for this. An important one was *custody of the eyes*. In ordinary language, keeping custody of the eyes meant minding your own business. In religious terms it involved a bit more. It meant keeping your eyes downcast, focused on the floor, never looking another person directly in the eye.

Failure to maintain custody of the eyes was called breaking custody, and this was considered a grievous fault. To make proper amends we had to ask the superior for a penance, usually some little act to perform which frequently included humiliation to make up for such failures and teach us to discipline our excessive and worldly desires.

This morning I was watching one of the local news programs. They are broadcasting from San Diego, and it was so nice to see the bay and the ocean. They also did shots from La Jolla. Just seeing people on the beach and the beautiful scenery of the many sailboats in Mission Bay made me want to be there so bad. San Diego is paradise to me. I would love to walk along the shore, feeling the water crash against my ankles and the sand between my toes, smelling the salty air, and listening to the sounds of the ocean. Absolute heaven! (Debra)

Custody of the hands meant never touching, and *custody of the body* meant no laughing or coughing, while *custody of the heart* meant keeping one's love for God alone. Eventually, we were taught that in order to become saints we would need to keep custody of everything and never let any reaction betray us.

I starve for human touch, but touching is forbidden. It is not done under any circumstances. The women here have gone to the hole over it. Two went for embracing. One had just gotten off the telephone with bad news, was crying, and needed a hug. They both did thirty days in the hole for sexual contact. Two others did hole time for sexual contact because one of the women untangled the other woman's hair curler. Of course, women have gotten write-ups for real sexual contact, but it's carried too far. Another example was two women who were talking and laughing. When one put her hand on the other's arm to tell her to stop what she was saying, you guessed it—to the hole. (Robin)

We were constantly warned about the dangers of *particular friendships*. At one point during my postulancy, I shared a room with three other women. Our beds had heavy iron frames with white curtains, which we tied back during the day and closed at night. For all practical purposes, with custody of the eyes, we never saw each other. One day, Mother Mistress called the four of us into her office and told us that we were going to be locked in our room at night because one of us was leaving and visiting someone down the hall after the lights were out. This was the sign of a particular friendship at its worst.

I can't go on. I am on the verge of going crazy or shooting myself. I have an excellent conduct record. I have never had a disciplinary action. In seven years, no one can say I have ever misbehaved. I only spoke with one other woman here, and Judy [Judy Buenoano, executed on March 30, 1998], may she rest in peace. (Ana)

Although I couldn't imagine then, or even now, who amongst us was guilty, I thought locking us in was hardly the solution. If we had been in the frame of mind to do so, we could have visited with each other all night behind locked doors. But no one asked my opinion. Fortunately, none of us were claustrophobic and no natural disaster occurred during our lockdown. We were never officially notified it was over, but one night, two weeks later, no one locked our door.

We all cope in different ways, and I have learned to cope by being alone. I cannot possibly explain what I feel psychologically, but I know that I only feel totally at ease in my room by myself. When I think about or know that I'm to be taken out of my room for some reason, I feel like a defenseless child who is about to be abused. (Debra)

The novices and professed sisters took care of small infractions of the Holy Rule in a type of public confession called the Chapter of Faults, from which postulants were spared. The Chapter of Faults took place on Friday evenings once a month.

At that time, each sister knelt before the community and confessed her offenses of the previous month. These could range from breaking dishes to being late for chapel.

I confessed. I said I did it. I call it loyalty. Love. Spouse, family, friends—you go bad for them. That's the way it is. The truth is the man always made advances to me. He attacked me, tried to more or less grope me, and my husband Billy walked in. He picked up a hammer and beat him in the head to death. I blacked out and don't remember a lot. The next day we were in the car. We were going to a wedding and Billy had to be fitted for a tuxedo. The body was in the trunk...or at least parts of it. (Kelley)

For many, the Chapter was a horrifying experience. Other members of the community were allowed and encouraged to accuse you of any offenses they had witnessed or you might have forgotten. Human nature being what it is, some used the occasion to get even. One went in, heart in hand, praying you hadn't offended anyone since the last Chapter.

For my part, once I became a novice and participated, I never bothered to accuse anyone besides myself since I was terribly distraught and could barely remember my own numerous failures at the time. It was fortunate that the Chapter was only once a month because even the stoics amongst us couldn't have taken it more.

I was taken out to Muncy Valley Hospital by two officers—at night, in the winter, in an ambulance after a fall.

There was three inches of snow on the ground and I had no coat or shoes. I was handcuffed, waist-chained, and shack-led the whole time and brought back by two officers who stopped the car in front of the Restricted Housing Unit. One of the officers walked twenty paces, then pulled his gun. This had never happened before. I not only feared my life, but was also humiliated and intimidated. There were four officers present, and I was not resisting, so pulling his gun was totally unnecessary and meant to scare me, I be-lieve. There were other staff present but nobody said any-thing or tried to stop it. (Kelley)

After a sister confessed, the superior was free to comment on what had been said or simply give a penance. One pen-ance she seemed fond of was having a sister kneel in the mid-dle of the chapel with her arms outstretched. There were often four or five of us kneeling this way at one time. We would be in the center of the marble aisle, in front of the community for at least twenty minutes.

The cuffing changed, and for showers and everything else we are cuffed behind our back. So trying to carry your towel, washcloth, soap, and shampoo is quite a task, and the team that gave us showers would not help at all. If we dropped something and couldn't pick it up, it stayed on the floor because they refused to pick it up. (Kelley)

Each day after lunch we were permitted one hour of recreation during which novices and postulants could talk to each other. These times were always charged with cumula-tive energy. People who'd wanted to converse for many days were allowed a few precious moments together. Because of this, everyone favored walks. We'd pair off in twos and the time shared together was priceless.

Those in charge were ever-vigilant for visible signs of particular friendships. One dead giveaway was spending all your walk time with the same person, or walking with the same partner two days in a row. If this was noticed, you were told who to walk with, in which case some other person's conversation with a friend might be interrupted to accommodate you. It wasn't unusual to find yourself paired off with someone you didn't care to know for a wasted hour while your inattentive mind was on someone else. But rules were rules, and more often than not we kept them.

I got really upset with the officers today because when we went to recreation, they would not allow me in the cage with Precious. At a time like this, she really needs someone near her, and she had told me yesterday that she wanted me to give her a hug. When I tried to go in the cage with her today they wouldn't allow me. They just don't want us to have any type of feelings for each other. I have been pouring love out that I didn't even know I had for the others here on the row with me. (Carolyn)

Once a month, on Sunday, we spent afternoon recreation writing letters. Since we were allowed to write only three letters a month, everyone had a good idea in advance who they'd be writing to. These letters were given unsealed to the superior. She read the letters we sent out as well as the letters we received. All incoming mail was opened.

In the state of Idaho, inmates cannot correspond with other inmates. The only exception is if it's a family member and you must submit a form that has to be approved by both facilities. We don't have a limit on letters, but on the number of envelopes you are allowed to purchase, which is twenty a week. You can use manila envelopes for attorney/

legal mail, so it could be over twenty letters that you send. Just recently we were told we can no longer use manila envelopes for personal correspondence. (Robin)

Postulants were allowed to read the mail we received once a week, but were only allowed to write only once a month. Novices received mail once a month and could write only once every three months.

If we received packages, they became part of the community supply closet from which our monthly allowance of soap, deodorant, toothpaste, writing paper, safety pins, and sanitary napkins was distributed to us.

If you are indigent, the prison will supply you with one envelope, eight sheets of paper, tooth powder, a bar of soap, and one pencil a week. Every three months a toothbrush. To qualify you must have less than one dollar in your account for sixty days. My sister sends me ten dollars every few months so I can buy hygiene products such as shampoo, conditioner, toothpaste, real soap, pen, paper, and envelopes. Every now and then someone else will send money in. Actually, although it says the prison supplies that stuff, they don't. The funds come out of the social recreation fund, and all monies in that come from the inmates. (Robin)

As postulants, we were permitted visitors on the first Sunday of every month. Novices were allowed visitors every three months. There was no limit to the number of people who could visit, but we couldn't leave the novitiate grounds. When the weather permitted, families took chairs outside and sat in large circles, laughing, talking, often eating and enjoying each other's company. I missed my family those days.

The prison approved my contact visits. I've been here one year and am now eligible for them. The warden said she wished she had five hundred inmates just like me. I had my first visit on July 5. It was great. My mom and sister came. I got to hug them. We sat at a table and talked. I felt normal for a little while. No glass, no cuffs. Just us. I could almost forget where I was—almost. (Christina)

When spring arrived, we were sent to be measured for our holy habits. This made it all very real. Each habit was made by a seamstress in the community and we were called almost daily for fittings. I was ecstatic. It was unbelievable to me—my dream was coming true. I would really be a nun.

The entire ordeal has been a nightmare of major proportions. It is so overwhelming that it is not possible for a normal, everyday citizen to understand. You would never imagine in your wildest dreams that any of this can happen to you. This happens to other people, or in the movies, and everyone would say, "Wow, how awful." Just imagine this happening to you and in this society. It can. (Debra)

The day a postulant is clothed in the religious habit for the first time, and becomes a novice, was called Reception Day in our community. Becoming a novice meant being accepted legally by the community and having the community receive you and assume responsibility for everything that happened during the novitiate year.

In preparation for Reception all the postulants went on an eight-day retreat. This meant we did not speak with anyone except a spiritual advisor, if we wished, during that period. It was a time to decide after two years of intense training whether or not this was the life for you.

Instead of me fighting to make death row better, I'm fighting to get off death row. And instead of me fighting to have material things, I'm fighting to have a life. A very long life off death row out of prison altogether. Back home with my eight- and eleven-year-old daughters where I belong. This is where my mind and heart is at—not on things and people that are not going to be any good to me here in prison on death row. (Donetta)

One of our group members left during the retreat. I didn't really notice at first, because if someone wasn't sitting or kneeling next to you, you might not. But another postulant wrote me an impulsive note saying she hadn't seen this particular person and asked if I thought she was sick. Although it was strictly forbidden, the two of us went to her room to find out.

We found her curtained bed made and her worn black shoes standing neatly next to it. Her freshly pressed postulant uniforms were in the tiny closet, and her thin black belt, silver medal, and small rosary were on the oak dresser. Everything was laid out like a frail memorial to something past. We knew, in one apprehensive glance, that she was definitely gone.

People who left were never discussed again. We weren't allowed to bring their names up in everyday conversations and we were forbidden to contact them in any way. Not only were they dead to us, but it was as if they had never existed at all.

Our unit has returned to its normal routine after Judy's execution. I find myself expecting to see Judy in her cell when I pass by on the way to shower. Staff has expressed the same feeling. I think it is habit from years of seeing her every day. Ana and I held a private good-bye and prayer for

Judy on the walkyard. (Virginia)

No woman who's entered a convent and stayed through Reception Day forgets it. Regardless of what course your life takes afterwards, it is a vivid memory that remains etched in one's soul. Ours dawned uncommonly foggy and damp. By 9:00 A.M. we were all in the oratory, where long shrouded tables had been set up and where each of us had a straight-backed chair with our bridal gown and veil draped over it. A pair of white heels stood like sentinels on the floor to complete the matrimonial ensemble. A professed sister was waiting to help each of us get dressed.

Some postulants had asked for particular nuns to dress them; in other cases, the nuns had made the request. Dressing a novice on her reception day was an honor, and usually any nuns who were related to the postulant participated in some way. Sister Thomasina helped me.

For two hours we primped and dressed and practiced walking and were taken to various locations throughout the house for pictures. We weren't allowed to see members of our family ahead of time. I didn't even know if mine was there.

Because of the court's actions and by Arizona Department of Corrections policy, I had to go through a mock execution. I had to sign papers about my last meal, witnesses I wanted present, how my remains would be disposed of. My veins were examined by a doctor, the chaplain stopped by for a visit, my room was searched every day, psychiatrists came around, and I was moved into an isolation cell where I could be watched continuously by a video camera. The experience was morbid and horrific, not to mention psychologically traumatizing. I agonized for days on end. (Debra)

From the time I entered the novitiate, I had been committed to the pursuit of perfection, and was quite relentless about it. I constantly challenged myself to go from one endless plateau to another, never fully satisfied with what I attained. It was, therefore, particularly difficult for me at the end of the year that I was one of the few who had not been requested for a mission.

I have come to realize that the justice system is not about justice at all, but about politics. It's sad and very frightening. Deep down in my heart I know that motives other than finding justice were instrumental in my conviction and sentencing. The trial itself was a miscarriage of justice, but the appeals process to which I am entitled proved even more alarming as to how "justice" is being practiced in real life. (Debra)

I grew more and more depressed as "accepting and adjusting" eluded me. It was dark and quiet in the chapel, and I went there for guidance. Shadows danced on the drab gray walls. I knelt down at St. Joseph's altar. There was a single white lily in a crystal vase standing before the likeness of the saint. In desperation, I prayed: *Lord, I'll go anywhere you ask, do anything you want. But, please, oh please, take me away from here.*

I hadn't expected an answer so soon, but in a matter of seconds the white lily wilted. I stared in disbelief as I watched it shrivel up and keel over. With any sense at all, I'd have taken it as a sign of things to come.

Part 2

Vespers

A
canonical
hour
of
psalms
of
thanksgiving
recited
in
the
evening

1.

At some point, I stopped thinking about Beth. She was a child when I knew her and, in a sense, so was I. But that didn't make it right. No one ever thought it was right. She was sixteen the summer I turned thirty-two. At her age I'd already entered the convent. By the time we met I'd never had a sexual experience and wasn't consciously looking for one. What I was looking for was another religious community.

I'd lived in South America for almost a decade as a nun and loved it. I reluctantly returned to the United States after the Allende years, at the beginning of Pinochet's coup. The American Catholic Church was still basically conservative; they weren't even close to where I had been. But some groups were moving faster than others. My community wasn't moving at all, though, and I grew restless. I missed the grassroots involvement.

Changing communities was not a usual practice in those days. Nuns who did change went from an active order to a cloistered order, or vice versa, but I knew of no one who went from one active order to another. Since there weren't any rules against it, I decided to try.

I'm the only female on death row in Arkansas. At the time I was sentenced they were not prepared for a death row inmate. The policies weren't even written until after I came. It is extremely lonely. I'm treated well, and I've been blessed with good officers. I'm sure I have it better than most. (Christina)

Despite the obvious misgivings of my community, I found a more progressive order and began teaching. Then I met Beth. She was a student in one of my classes, and when I look at students now I can't explain, not even to myself, how we became lovers. Yet we did, though we never shared a bed.

I spend my time reading and rocking myself to sleep. I roll my blanket up and hug it. It's all I need, really. I'm no lesbian. I exercise in my cell. I eat, I stand around, I sometimes shoot the shit with the girls. We're always locked down in our cells. (Kelley)

There must have been something special about her, but I don't remember particularly noticing her until the day she came to Spanish class dissolved in tears. Nothing had been right since her parents' recent divorce was how she explained it.

She was tall, athletic, and wore glasses. Basketball was her game of choice—her number was twenty-two. She called herself the leader. Her job was to build team spirit, not score points. She ran fifty laps a day and broke several records in track.

I am still here on death row and I spend a lot of time just standing in my cell looking out of the peephole. At first I tried to get things changed. I'd talk to the other women about different things. But I've gotten tired of writing stuff up, writing the ACLU. What's the point, really? Life on death row is all about the hardest kind of punishment. You can see for yourself. There's a bunk, a footlocker, a chair, a TV over the toilet. We can't keep anything on the walls. It's a pretty monotonous life. There are no programs, and we're not allowed to work. So I'm in my cell all the time except for showers and when they let us out in the yard. (Andrea)

One day I found a brown paper bag from the local supermarket under my desk with a note attached: *To the sunshine of my life.* In it was a blue sweatshirt, my size, with the number twenty-two on the back. I'd never been the sunshine in anyone's life.

The tremendous amount of pain, guilt, and regret I live with every day is just too much. I can't live any longer with what I've done and without my babies. I love and miss them very much. They were the only joy and sunshine in my life. (Christina)

She was smart, idealistic, and loved words. We talked incessantly. She had questions about everything. Her boyfriend's name was Tony. Around school he was called The Fonz. She had several younger brothers and an older sister. Her sister, a senior—Space was her nickname—was on drugs. Beth was the responsible one. She nurtured, and did it well.

I talked to my son and daughter on Saturday. They are such wonderful children, and I thank the Creator every day for them. Even though I am not with them now they are doing fine. I know they have a void in their lives, just as I have in mine being away from them, but the values that I tried to instill in them—I guess they do care and learned to respect people. I always wanted them to know how important life is in any form. Yes, without a doubt, they are what helps me go on in every way. Otherwise, I would truly give up. Because any day or time that I can see them or talk to them—I never want to miss that with them. (Carolyn)

Grades were important. She knew she could get a scholarship to go to college. She never missed an assignment or class. She wanted to make something of her life. I liked that about her. She was always on the run, rushing to prepare a meal, trying to come up with enough money to buy peanut butter, wondering why her little brother kept coughing at night. Her mother was seldom home. Beth had a strong faith in God.

My faith in God has given me the strength to face each day on death row. I dealt with it better when my sons were small because I kept telling myself that I still had time to spend with them because I would be free before they grew up. But now it is painful knowing all the time and precious moments have been missed, that they have grown up without me. They are young men now, and I realize we've lost all those years.

My boys are seventeen and eighteen now, but when I came in they were just little. And I know this sounds like a small thing, but I can't even tell you what size shoes my oldest wears. You know what I'm saying? I don't know what size shirts they wear or their favorite foods. And these are the kinds of things a mother wants to know. I just want to go home. Please understand what I'm saying. I could never do enough time to replace human life. There's nothing I can do to bring that police officer back. But I have given him fourteen years of my life. What is the sense of keeping me here? (Andrea)

It happened slowly between us. She liked to play and enjoyed saying things that shocked me—things I'd never heard before. Things for which I had no response. She said she loved my ears. She'd tell me I had the most beautiful ears with the tiniest lobes and write poems about them. I was flattered beyond remorse. She'd cut out pictures of different people and paste them on brightly colored construction paper with I LOVE EARS written on the top, then leave them on my desk. I discovered I had ears and was both amused and surprised.

As I grew up I became overweight. I was put down by my stepmother about my weight and subjected to comments that my dad would do nothing about. Some family members would tell me how to lose weight, or tell me how pretty I would be if I was thinner, but I continued to gain weight. Food became my friend, especially when I was upset. At times I would eat until I was sick, hoping that the food would make me feel better. Usually it did, but it also compounded the problem. I became so sensitive that I began to believe I was less of a person because of my weight. A person who would never be popular, date, or just plain fit in. (Christina)

And she noticed little things about me, like when my "green eyes were sad." She wanted me to know the people, places, and things that were meaningful to her, and I wanted her to know my meanings, too. Together we were ageless. If I'd had a rough day, or if I was worried and tired, she'd know right away. I was amazed at that.

One person told me, "I feel so bad when I see you in here. Your head is always down and there is such a sadness in your eyes. I see that you are suffering, but the one who should be suffering is your friend." Then I tell them, "Only God knows what she is doing and God will treat her accordingly." (Ana)

She copied long quotations about friendship and love onto little pieces of paper I'd find stuck in my books. The lyrics of love songs were taped inside my desk drawers. Or I'd walk into my classroom to teach and I LOVE YOU would be scrawled in giant letters across the board. There was no question who had written it. I'd never known a student quite like her.

No one can imagine how the heart can hurt. The pain grows deeper each day, and I wonder how much more pain a person can endure. It has become a daily struggle to hang on to human values. I believe in human values, but do the people who are in power get to decide over life and death? Even more important, do they care about safeguarding a life beyond any reasonable doubt, as our constitution prescribes? I seriously wonder about that. (Debra)

At times she'd walk by me and brush against me ever so lightly and I'd feel a warmth shoot through me in a thousand directions. Or she'd come up behind my desk and playfully kiss me on top of the head and I'd want to turn around and suck her up into me whole, just the way she was.

She said things like, "You dig?" or, "I spaced him off nicely today." Her favorite greeting was, "Hey, hey, hey." She loved biblical names like Jeremiah, Isaiah, and Jedediah, and together we named most of the trees in town.

I'm a very spiritual person. I know that God gives me unconditional love that keeps me going from day to day. I pray daily, and God is very important in my life. Every morning when I wake up in my cell the first thing I do is pray. Then I do my bible studies and write letters. After I was saved, I began signing the letters I wrote Life Row *instead of* Death Row. *(Andrea)*

We touched and kissed and my body came alive. We had names for each other. I called her sunshine, and she called me her green-eyed-Irish-babe. And we had words and looks that were only ours. A language all our own.

She was the first person to touch me between my legs and I loved her touch. It drove me crazy, and when it happened I prayed it would never end. One day she opened me and gently touched me with her warm tongue. I felt this beautiful tremor well up inside and ripple through me and I thought I would die. It was an awakening I'd never dreamt of. Suddenly I had a body, I had needs and wants, I had desires. I flowed. I was alive and ridiculously happy.

The first time I was with a woman I was twelve and she was thirty-eight years old. I had no idea what I was doing, really, but she knew and she knew how to make me feel so good. At twelve years old I was very mature for my age. I always knew I liked girls because I had been doing things with my little girlfriends since I was about six years old— and I know that I didn't look at the boys that way. (Carolyn)

We wrote long sensuous letters and made love over the phone and came to each other over and over again. We went on hikes and rode bikes and had picnics by the lake, and she jogged miles to see me almost every day. I gave her a ring which she always wore on "the strongest finger of my strongest hand on my strongest arm." And she had a life with Tony, too. And we were like that for about three months.

My parents found out about me and other women. They also found letters that Mary had written to me. My mother could not believe it, and my parents never talked about it with me until about four years later. By this time I was seeing her on a regular basis and getting ready to move in with her. And they had so many questions, like, "Who is this woman?" and, "What do you do together?" I mean, really different things than you would imagine parents would ask. Now I talk very openly to my parents about other women. (Carolyn)

Then one day her mother called. She invited me to their house. "A prayer meeting," she said, and in a way it was. Her family was all there. I looked at Beth, she looked away. Her mother read from the bible: "Woe to those who give scandal to little children. It would be better for them to have a millstone tied around their neck and be thrown in the ocean and drowned." I listened quietly, not understanding.

I did not understand what was said in my trial. The translator told me it was not important, and the lawyers I had did not speak Spanish. The judge never allowed evidence in my favor. Ultimately he told me that if he saw me crying I would be taken out of the courtroom. (Ana)

She told me why they had gathered. She'd found my letters, my precious letters to Beth. Invisible hands grasped me by the throat and slowly began to squeeze. I tried to stand but my legs were gone.

The terror and fear inside was overwhelming. First of all, in the midst of the shock and all the emotions I was feeling knowing I didn't do anything, I couldn't understand why I was going to jail. I knew I was innocent, so I asked if I could go home. Of course, the judge told me I couldn't. (Debra)

Her demands were simple. I would resign my teaching position and leave the school the following day. The district attorney had my letters. If I refused to do this I'd be charged with a felony. Beth wouldn't return to school until I was gone.

By some miracle I walked out of her house that night. I was dazed. I wanted to scream. I wanted to say, *It was love.* My mind raced. Who could I tell? Where would I go? How do nuns resign? What about Beth—what did she think? What does a district attorney do? And what is a felony?

Mostly my lawyer didn't have a defense for me. For a while they thought they would say I had PMS. They constantly were doing tests, drawing enough blood out of me to make another person. My lawyer thought they were going to charge me with second-degree murder. When he found out it was murder in the first, well, he only had two months to prepare the case. He told the judge that I was competent to stand trial, that I understood the facts in my case, but I didn't. (Andrea)

That night I felt weak and scared. She'd said I was sick. A homosexual. Could that be true? And if I was, why couldn't God have given me a more acceptable disease? Is there even a cure, I wondered, or must I be punished for the rest of my life? I tried to organize my thoughts. I'd resign the next day, then Beth could go back to school. That much I could do for her.

The convent was dark when I got home, the sisters were all in bed. I knew I had to call my superior that night. There was a phone booth in the convent dining room where you could close the door and a light would go on. It was an eerie feeling sitting in there looking out at the darkened room. Someone had made a book of tunes you could play by touching certain numbers on the phone. It dangled limply before me on a silken string. I picked it up and slowly punched out the notes for the song on the first page: *Three blind mice, three blind mice, see how they run....* My hands were shaking uncontrollably. Finally, I made my call.

For months before my sentence was handed down I tried to prepare myself for the death sentence I felt I'd receive. Although I thought I was ready, when the judge actually said it my knees buckled, my eyes welled up with tears, and I started to shake uncontrollably. (Robin)

As soon as I spoke she told me she'd already heard, that

Beth's mother had called her. She didn't repeat what had been said to her. She didn't ask if I had an explanation or anything to add. I was too afraid to ask questions. She said she'd made an appointment for me to see the bishop the next day. I wondered why; I didn't even know him. She told me to go to school in the morning and sign resignation papers, then teach my class until 11:00 A.M. when someone would drive me to my meeting with the bishop.

Control of my life began to slip away. I hung up the phone and sat in the booth almost until daylight. That night, and for many years to come, I slept very little.

They have total control of my life. They tell me when to get up, when to go to bed, when my bed has to be made, when I eat, when I shower, what I wear, when I go to recreation, and on and on. I have no privacy. (Robin)

I drove to school as usual in the morning, in the convent car with the other nuns. No one knew. I went to the principal's office. He knew. Beth's mother and aunt were there to see to it that I kept my word. The papers were waiting. They stated I was resigning for personal reasons. No one asked me what they were. He showed me where to sign.

Beth's aunt looked at me and said, "You look just like all those homos." I was stunned. I felt a knife begin to turn. I was certain I deserved whatever was said, I knew I was slime. Somewhere inside, though, I couldn't help but wonder what all those "homos" looked like.

There are so many different twists in this scenario— anger, jealousy, hatred, revenge—each with their own meaning behind them, either self-serving or pure vindictiveness. You are being portrayed by the media as an evil woman who wanted her child killed when all you tried to do is to protect him from the evil that surrounded you. That you are evil is on the news every day, but down deep inside you know you are not that kind of person. (Debra)

Beth's mother insisted I'd have to get out of town, warning me not to contact any students I knew before I left. She hadn't said this before. I felt helpless in the face of her fury as if hands were at my throat trying to strangle me. I could hardly breathe. I looked at my watch and realized I still had two hours to teach.

Sometimes I don't have any strength and feel I am drowning in pain. Every day is worse. I feel like I can't breathe. I don't see how I will ever get a new trial. This woman did so much harm to my children and me. She destroyed the life of an innocent child to get revenge on me. Why didn't she kill me instead? But she told me, "I'll destroy you, I'll do something you will never forget." This I will never forget. (Ana)

I went to my classroom a zombie, almost an empty shell. Those were the two longest hours of my teaching career. I looked at each student and longed to say good-bye. I didn't want to just disappear from their lives. I was drowning in grief.

"Sister, can I hand this in on Monday?" Jessica asked.

"Sure, Monday will be fine," I replied.

"Sister, are we still having that quiz on Friday?" Paul wanted to know.

"Yes. of course, we are," I assured him.

"Hey, Sis, you don't look so good," David reminded me.

My emotions remain on a roller coaster today [the day of Judy Buenoano's execution] as I say good-bye to Judy in my heart. I don't judge her past but accept the person I have known for four and a half years. A friend that helped me adjust to "living" on death row, someone that eased the daily pain with laughter. (Virginia)

At 10:50, I told my class to study and left the room. The sister who drove me to the chancery never spoke and neither did I. I didn't know what anyone knew.

The bishop said he regretted these events. Since he explained nothing, I assumed he meant my leaving. I felt humiliated and cried.

I am very ashamed of what happened and every day I regret it. It is bad enough to be known as a mother who killed her own babies without people knowing how it was done. They don't want to and can't understand how out of touch with reality I was that night. Otherwise this never would have happened—I loved Justin and Shelby so much, I'd never intentionally hurt them. They were all I had, but I don't ever expect society as a whole to understand or try to because I have learned that it is easier to see the difference than the likeness. (Christina)

Then I asked him to hear my confession. I wanted forgiveness even as I wondered how sickness can be forgiven. He told me no, he couldn't risk being involved in a scandal. I hated him for that, and in that moment I gave up my faith.

My grandmother keeps telling me to have faith. Well, some of those who were executed also had faith and some of those who didn't still turned their lives over to God. Some innocent, some not. I have faith and I know God understands my decision. And isn't the important thing that He knows I didn't do it, and I know it, so it doesn't matter what others think? (Kelley)

That same afternoon the superior told me to move out of the convent. I was both shocked and terrified: I had been in a convent since I was a senior in high school, almost twenty years. I had no place to go and no money to go there with. She said that officially I was still in the process of changing from one community to another, and that theoretically I didn't belong to them—a "fact" that hadn't been mentioned during my four years of living there. It wasn't likely that my previous community would want me back in the midst of a scandal either. I'd never felt so alone, torn in every direction. I felt love and hatred, anger and fear, worry, shame, guilt, and terrible, terrible grief.

I want a judge to know my pain and grief. I want someone to ask him how much longer I must wait until I can grieve properly for my son. For eight years I've been fighting this system, and I have yet to grieve. I wasn't even allowed to attend my only child's funeral. I want this judge to acknowledge that this was a personal tragedy. I want him to acknowledge the outrage of what this state put me through. I sometimes think if I could stand before the judge, I'd pour my heart and soul out to him. I wouldn't talk that legal mumbo jumbo. I'd make him see what happened. I'd make sure he could see my pain. (Debra)

I didn't want to go home. My mother was in her eighties. What could I tell her? I didn't understand what was happening myself.

I called a retreat house owned by the community I'd been in first, the one I suddenly still belonged to. I told them who I was and said I wanted to go there for a week or so. I thought that if I could get away, I would be able to think, to figure things out and then take it from there. At first they said it was all right, but later they called back and said it wasn't "advisable." Fortunately, I didn't know then that this was only the beginning.

Many people have harmed me. Television and newspapers have made me out to be the worst. People from the press have sent me letters asking to interview me—even TV channels—but I never answer their letters, much less give them an interview. The press doesn't care about feelings. They are only interested in the sensational. Something the public will read and will give them a name. They don't care if a person is suffering or whether they are telling the truth or lies. They play with your pain and desperation. We are a story to them. But my pain and suffering is not a made-up story—it is real. I don't want anyone playing with my pain. (Ana)

I typed a letter to the sisters I lived with. I couldn't leave without saying good-bye. The superior had admonished me to tell no one, so I gave no explanations. I merely said I'd decided to leave. I said that I loved them, and I did. I taped the letter to the refectory door just before I walked out for the last time.

One of my sons found out about my death warrant being signed in the newspaper. He was only eight years old when it happened and nobody thought he knew anything about what was going on. He was in his classroom reading the newspaper and there it was. He can still remember it as if it just happened. (Andrea)

In Chile, I had had a student in one of my high school English classes who eventually married a North American. They lived in Ohio. She told me once, "Sister, if you ever need anything, anything at all, just call me."

Beth had given me the only money I had. She'd sent it through her sister who passed it to me under the divider between two bathroom stalls in a Pizza Hut. It was $260, money Beth had been saving since the second grade. I felt bad taking it but I had nothing else. I bought my ticket to Marcela's.

I stayed with Marcela and her husband for three months. They never asked why I had come, and I never told them. I only said I was sick. Every day I'd sit on the couch and cry. Marcela and her husband would both kiss me when they left for work in the morning, and when they'd come home I'd still be there. I cried for weeks. I couldn't stop. Great waves of pain would come from the pit of my stomach and my whole body would ache. I contacted my mother and told her I'd taken some time off. I promised I'd be home to see her soon.

I was still in total denial as to what happened to my son. I remember being housed in the psychiatric unit of the Durango jail and having several psychiatrists come to visit me on a regular basis. I was suffering from severe depression, shock, and hour-long crying spells. I was treated with antidepressants all the way into my trial days. My depression was not the result of being incarcerated, of having lost my freedom. It was the loss of my son—the only thing left in my shattered life—that just overwhelmed me. (Debra)

Before I left, I'd rented a post office box in my own name in the town where Beth lived. I managed to send the key to her. It was a risk, I realized that. Yet I had to know she was all right. I wrote painful letters to her daily, then addressed them to myself and mailed them. Beth would ride her Schwinn bike, the one she'd named Jedediah, to the post office and pick them up. She'd go to the park, read the letters till she knew them by heart, tear them in tiny pieces, and stuff them down a city drain.

And some days she'd call me from a phone booth outside the school and stand there and cry, and I'd want to reach into the wires to find her and cradle her in my arms.

Sometimes I can't think about them. It's like they're being ripped away from me all over again. Every day I wonder why this tragedy has happened. I am not someone who is content with the answer, Sometimes there are no answers. I believe there is a reason for everything. I am having a very difficult time rationalizing why this had to happen. I know life isn't fair. I know life isn't predictable. I have tried to learn from the incidents in my past. But I cannot figure out what I am supposed to learn, what can be so valuable for me to learn that it had to cost the lives of two children? (Christina)

Beth's mother also called me. She said she'd hired a detective who would be following me wherever I went. She wanted to know where I was at all times. I was terribly afraid of her. She threatened me and my family. I thought she was capable of anything.

I couldn't talk to anyone, male or female, because she felt I was talking about her. If I left the house she beat me. All my friends distanced themselves from me because they didn't want problems with her. And when she got drunk it was even worse. I lived in hell—she did so many things to me. I was terribly afraid of her. (Ana)

2.

In April I stopped crying. I called my mother and said I'd

be home for Easter. I knew it was important for me to set goals.

I decided I had to stop and see Beth on the way. It was foolish, but I had to know: I was crazy thinking I had destroyed her life.

You cannot imagine how I am suffering. Every day I cry tears of desperation, tears of pain, tears of torture. I never thought she would be so vengeful, but I am paying for a crime I didn't do. This has destroyed my heart. Pain is now my life. (Ana)

The bus I took to my mother's house passed through the town where Beth lived. We planned to spend a few minutes together at the depot. It seemed so simple.

I knew there was a bus change. But just before we arrived the driver told me I wouldn't be able to get another bus until the next morning. This was not something I'd planned. Although I was nervous about staying overnight in that town, I had no choice. I'd find a cheap motel.

I spotted her immediately when the bus pulled in. She was across the street from the station sitting on her bike. It had been three months, but she looked much younger than I remembered. She probably looked her age. I knew then I shouldn't have returned.

Beth met me inside the depot. She was jittery and high-strung, not the bubbly, carefree person I'd committed to memory. She stayed with me for only a few minutes, then I sent her away. We were both stretched to the point of breaking. We held each other and cried. I don't remember saying good-bye. I never saw her again.

I've made some bad choices, I'll admit that. I started drinking and I used drugs. I was a go-go dancer. I fenced stolen items. But I was a good mother. I always watched after my kids and provided for them. Experience makes you look back and see your mistakes. If I ever do get out, this is always going to be my past. I probably wouldn't be able to be back with my kids, but I would want more kids, one or two. I'd move out of Pennsylvania, go out West, find a real job— not as a stripper. Maybe I'd get married again. You know, have a family, a job, the whole Brady Bunch thing. (Kelley)

Alone in a seedy motel in a hostile town, my money almost gone, I impulsively called a student from the high school who had a car and asked her to pick me up in the morning and drive me to the bus station. She said it would be no problem.

I put my luggage outside the motel door the following morning and watched TV while waiting for Cory. A car drove up. The lot was mostly empty. It wasn't Cory. It was Beth's mom and two other women I didn't know. They were getting out of the car with bibles in their hands. All the blood seemed to drain out of me. I was frozen to the spot. Those hands were at my throat again. They knocked at the door, and I let them in.

As soon as they sat down a part of me drifted away. I found myself somewhere above us, looking down on the entire scene. It felt peaceful but strange. I heard what they were saying, but it didn't matter. A part of me wanted to stay up there.

I've been having a lot of out-of-body experiences lately, and what I mean by that is I am here and I can see and hear all that is going on around me, but it's like I am not really here. I sleep all day and have all kinds of strange dreams and then I stay up most of the night because there is no sound around me and the out-of-body feelings finally stop.

But only when everyone else is sleeping. Do you think I am losing it? (Carolyn)

All too soon I was back. They'd come to speak about my sickness, they said. They'd found a list in my desk at school. Girls' names. Maybe twenty. Had I been "that way" with all of them? The girls would have to take lie detector tests and the truth would be known. Of course, I would also have to be tested. I had no idea what they were talking about. Their words flew at me like darts, then bounced off. Nothing could hurt me anymore. I had reached my limit, I'd stepped over the threshold. I felt no pain. They were reading from their bibles of Sodom and Gomorrah and asking if I wanted to be healed. They assured me that they still loved me as a child of God. Then they began to pray.

I ask God to forgive the people who have been cruel to me because they do not know what they are doing. I ask God to give me strength and to care for my son who will live eternally in my heart. If I knew that my son could live again, nothing else would matter. I would cut off my legs, or even sell my soul to the devil if this were possible, to make my son, Lazarito, live again. I have carried this pain for years. She won. She had her vengeance. She took what would hurt me most—my children—and even now she continues to do us harm. (Ana)

Meanwhile, Cory arrived. She knocked, and when I answered the door I told her I couldn't leave, though thinking back, I don't know why I said that. She took my luggage with her and assured me she'd be back. Beth's mother insisted I'd have to go with them; she'd made an appointment for me. I thought she meant with the district attorney. Instead, she said it was with a shrink. There were arrangements for me to stay with the two women who were with her for as long as my therapy lasted. My mind was boggled. This woman had taken over my life. Then the three of them suggested we have lunch. They joked and made small talk over tortillas and chips while I was dying inside. I wanted to run. It was all so bizarre.

I felt at the edge of my sanity. When we reached the main police station, he walked me inside and we took an elevator to his office. Then he asked if I wanted a soda. I said yes, and that I also wanted to talk to my dad. I was refused. I remember all these bright lights and cameras. I was in shock and did not understand anything going on around me. I also remember him taking me on a tour through his office bragging about his certificates and awards.

He continued with his accusations in such a vile manner that I started screaming at him. "Look," I cried, "I am not a crazy person! I am not an animal! I am not capable of doing anything of what you are steadily accusing me of. I want to know what happened to my son." Nothing made any sense to me. (Debra)

The church ladies' apartment was small for two. I couldn't imagine the three of us there for any length of time. We sat and looked at each other in silence until they said they had to leave and would be back in a couple of hours. I had no intention of being there when they returned.

As soon as they left I called the bus depot. No more buses that day. It didn't matter I'd go somewhere, anywhere. I had to get away. I called a taxi and told them to hurry. An emergency, I said. The cab arrived just as the women returned. They didn't notice it as they approached the front door. I sat on the couch until they came in and went to the other room to hang up their coats. Then I opened the door and left. I ran down the sidewalk, jumped in the taxi, and locked all the doors. The driver eyed me through the mirror. I can't imagine what he must have thought. A nun who looked so afraid.

One of the women ran out and tried to open the cab door. She told the driver to let her in. He pulled away instead. She yelled at me that I'd regret the day I left, but I never have.

A lot of regret, that's what goes through my mind, day in, day out—God's punishing me. He let me live so I would suffer. I know it sounds crazy, but the torture I put myself through every day is more than you can imagine. (Christina)

I had the driver take me to the same motel where I stayed the night before. I didn't know any other and was too frightened to think clearly. They gave me a different room. I was shaking so hard I could barely hold the pen to sign my name.

Once inside the room I locked the door and sat in the dark for several hours, unable to move. I knew they were after me. I was on the run, more terrified than I'd ever been. I still don't know how I survived that night.

Florida houses the five of us in a segregation unit—X dorm for Xecution. We are locked down twenty-four hours a day, handcuffed for the ten-minute shower three times a week and the two hours allowed outside per week. The only contact is the brief nod or hello from the officer who places the food tray through the slot at 6:00 and 11:00 A.M., and 4:00 P.M. The overhead light remains on around the clock for visual contact at all times. (Virginia)

Cory had my luggage. After sitting immobilized for a few hours, I was able to call the store where she worked and ask her to come the following morning for a replay of the day before. I wanted to press her not to tell anyone where I was, but I didn't.

Later that night, around 9:00 P.M., the telephone in the motel room rang. The sound seemed frighteningly loud and menacing. Who knew where I was? Was it one of the women I'd just escaped from? Was it Beth's mom? Had Cory told someone? When I finally answered and heard Cory's voice, I tried to slow my racing heart.

As far as phone calls go they have reduced our calls from three a week to one. I can understand how that might work with two hundred men wanting to use the telephone. But we are four women and all mothers. I know that some men on death row are fathers, but women are the ones who keep in close contact with our children. I have three children who live in Virginia and two in Oklahoma. The new policy means that each week I have to choose between my children and have no calls to anyone else. It is already difficult for my children to know that their mother is on death row. Is there a reason I will be denied even telephone access? (Carolyn)

There was a warrant out for my arrest, she told me. She didn't know why, they hadn't said. Everyone had been warned to notify the police if they heard from me. My mind exploded. I'd never imagined I'd end up like this. They hadn't explained what a felony was when they told me I'd be charged with one. I thought they were after me because I had returned to town and in my mind I tried to figure out if that actually was a crime. Would they handcuff me and take me to jail? Did I have any rights?

Even then I couldn't believe they really wanted me. It was a horrible nightmare that seemed to get worse. Homosexuality was a sin, I knew, but was it a crime? I had no grasp on the world's realities. I couldn't imagine a nun going to jail, much less imagine that I was that nun.

Imagine living your normal day to day life. You don't break the law. You work for a living trying to support yourself and your child. You have a friend that you have known for a few years, and this friend treats you with respect and concern. You do things together like going out for pizza, shopping—all the things friends do. One day your friend asks to borrow your car because his is not working and he wants to go shopping. Your child wants to go along. You say it's all right because, after all, your child knows your friend and you trust your friend.

Hours later your friend calls to tell you your child has been kidnapped. There is mass confusion and hysteria. You are sick with worry and anguish and you can't sleep, eat, or even think straight. You are up for hours and trying to help the police as best as you can and, in the meantime, your mind can't help but think the worst. You imagine your child being hurt by a child molester, or even drugged. You go through so many emotions all at once at the same time that you are trying to be helpful with the police. After thirty hours have gone by, you are literally drained both emotionally and physically. The next day you are wanted by the police for questioning. You think for sure your child was found and that the police are going to reunite you. (Debra)

Cory said she hadn't told them where I was and didn't think she should. She told me she was coming to the motel that night, that I didn't sound good, and that maybe I shouldn't be alone. I begged her not to come, but she came anyway with a friend. She said they were both eighteen and spent many nights away from home. No one would be concerned. I was concerned, but I didn't turn them away.

The three of us sat on my bed all night, mostly in silence, mostly in the dark. I was grateful for their presence. Periodically my despair threatened to overwhelm me and I'd start to cough, gasping for air. I'd shake whenever a car drove into the lot and couldn't make myself stop. I hated being so out of control. Sometimes I tried to talk, but what was there to say?

In my attempts to hide what happened to me as a child and not deal with my feelings, I blocked the events from my memory for many years. But the emotions stayed with me. I grew up constantly feeling different, ashamed and guilty, and believed that no one really understood me. I guess maybe because I didn't understand my own feelings.

Somewhere along the way I became afraid of showing my emotions to others. I never told people when I was mad or hurt because of them or their actions. I thought that if I told them and they didn't agree or like what I said, they would get mad at me, and I didn't want that. I hated confrontation. It was easier to agree and hide my ideas and feelings than to express them and risk rejection or making them mad. I don't know when or why I started to feel this way. It just seemed to be part of me. (Christina)

Finally, it was morning. I only wanted to leave, but there were two hours before my bus and Cory insisted she had to stop home before dropping me off. She was always home for breakfast after a night away, she said. When we pulled up at her house I wanted to stay in the car, but her mother came out and invited me in for a cup of coffee while Cory drove her friend home. A simple act of kindness was enough to make me cry.

I had something happen in my family once and I cried for days, I was so distraught. I am only allowed two rolls of bathroom tissue a week and I ran out because of my crying and needed another roll. The male officer asked why. I am frightened of this particular officer and I couldn't answer him. He came back to my cell and gave me a lecture on waste. At about that time the sergeant walked back to my cell and saw me crying. When he asked what was up, the officer told him. The sergeant said, "Give her a roll, she's having a rough time right now." I thanked him, and he stayed with me until I could bring myself under control. A little human kindness isn't hard to give. (Robin)

Too much time passed and Cory had not yet returned. The pit of my stomach said something was wrong. I sat at the upright piano that stood next to the kitchen door and tried to calm myself by playing, but my fingers only shook across the keys. When Cory's car drove up I saw out of the corner of my eye that she wasn't in it. Three people got out: the principal of the high school, the sheriff, and a priest.

I ran to the hall bathroom, locked the door, and stood there not knowing what to do. I knew I couldn't hide in the bathroom, yet there was no place left to go. They knocked and asked for me by name. As I emerged, my legs trembling uncontrollably, I saw the sheriff and was certain I was headed to jail. Once I accepted that, I made up my mind to be dignified and went to the living room and sat on the couch.

Reality set in as we drove through those prison gates. When I heard them close behind me, in my mind I knew I was trapped forever. I couldn't turn around and say, "Open sesame." I was in prison, and I was going to death row. Me, yes, really me. (Robin)

The priest asked Cory's mother to leave. He told her to go visit one of her neighbors even though she was standing in her own house. I asked her to stay. I barely knew her, but I was afraid to be alone with those men. I was so frightened by all the unknowns. She left without a word.

The sheriff said they were taking me to the bus. I had to leave town immediately and never come back. I almost laughed, I was so relieved. They were not going to arrest me. The principal called the bus depot and asked when the next bus to anywhere was leaving. They escorted me to the depot in silence. Several people were milling about, waiting for the same bus I would be on. When it arrived my three escorts got on the bus with me in case I tried to run. They got off without saying a word after I was seated. I don't know what the rest of the people thought.

We commandeered a rest stop, a gas station, because I had to use the toilet. It was on the way back to prison after receiving a stay of execution. People were sitting around, you know, pumping gas, and in we all come. They had shotguns and stuff. They made people inside the mini-mart stop what they were doing and stand up against the wall. It was like a television movie or something. Then I walked in shackled, handcuffed, and chained. I mean, I was chained up. The only place I didn't have a chain was around my neck. All this just so I could take a pee. I'm sure everyone was wondering, God, what did she do? (Andrea)

Tears blurred the buildings and streets we passed as the bus pulled out. I tried to control them but couldn't. The dam was overflowing. At the first place we stopped I got information about the bus schedule home. I had several hours to wait at the depot. At least I was safe. I felt safe in crowds.

The darkness and despair overwhelms me. It gets to the point when my little cell becomes my haven, where I'm safe, at least for a little bit. (Robin)

3.

I arrived at my mother's house that night and almost immediately made out a schedule for myself. I felt secure in routines. They were my lifeline.

I put a sign on my bedroom mirror—DEAR SADNESS, PLEASE GO AWAY—which I read aloud each morning and night. I started doing things by numbers: one, put your feet on the floor; two, get out of bed; three, go to the bathroom, and on and on.

I went to Mass daily and took Communion, too. The familiar rituals were soothing. And when I walked back from the Communion rail I forced myself to hold my head up and look forward, rather than keep my eyes down as I'd been taught. I had to know I was in control of something.

I spent mornings at the public library. In the afternoons I rode my bike to the park. There I claimed a table where I could write and cry. This kept me breathing. I missed Beth and knew nothing of her. I was wracked with guilt thinking of the devastation I'd caused in her young life. Had she even survived? Sometimes I wanted her just to be able to experience the sense of intimacy I'd learned. Sometimes I ached all over. On most days, my tears played havoc with the words I wrote.

This is my schedule: breakfast 6:30; lunch 11:30; dinner 4:45. It's on a tray, brought to me. Beverage with breakfast only. Food is usually cold, but not always. Pill call 6:00 A.M. and 8:00 P.M. Medication dispenses and medical requests picked up. Nurse comes to my room.

Lights on at 6:00 A.M. and off at 10:00 P.M. This doesn't mean I have to go to bed. If I want I can stay up all night. Being isolated and alone, I can't disturb anyone, so no one cares.

Room cleaning days are Tuesday and Thursday. Laun-

dry days are Monday and Thursday. There is one hour of recreation daily, which must be finished by 4:00 P.M.

Daily showers are in the mornings. Supplies are given out in mornings. Commissary items are delivered on Monday. Forms must be in by Wednesday. (Robin)

One day when I returned from the park my mother told me a priest had called. I tried to hide my alarm. He called back, and I realized it was the same priest who had escorted me to the bus. I was flooded with terror when I heard his voice. I had thought I'd be safe at home and would never hear from him again. He said we needed to talk, that it was official, and if I refused he'd come to my home.

We met at the Holiday Inn the next day. Across cups of black coffee he told me Beth's mother had decided to press charges unless I agreed to see a psychiatrist. He showed me two typed letters from the district attorney's office detailing the charges of child molesting and sodomizing a minor. I had no idea what sodomizing a minor meant, but child molesting was clear. That was the first time I'd really understood. The penalties were also listed: ten to twenty years in prison for one; twenty-five to life for the other. There was nothing about love or caring on the papers. That this document applied to me was almost inconceivable. When I saw it in black and white I felt like a monster.

It has always amazed me that the prosecutor could say the things he said about me when he didn't even know me. I once mentioned that to my trial attorneys and was told that if the prosecutor spent five minutes with me, I would become human to him and he couldn't effectively prosecute me. (Robin)

I agreed to see a psychiatrist. I had no choice. The priest

accompanied me that very day to one he picked out of the yellow pages. He went in first and talked. When he came out he said the doctor would see me, but if I missed any appointments the psychiatrist would call him and they would proceed with the criminal charges. My life was no longer my own. I signed the papers and left.

My mind has changed since the last time we spoke and after the appeal. I am waiving the rest of my appeals. I am tired, and I just hope these letters that I am writing will help someone in the future, even if not me. (Carolyn)

I hated the psychiatrist and his power. I told him as little as I could. He wanted the only things that were still mine— my thoughts and memories of Beth. Each appointment was more painful than the one before. He pried. *When did we do it? How many times? Did I like any part of her body more than the rest? What turned me on?* His questions were despicable. I had never spoken about sex with anyone. I didn't even have the words. He said my therapy would take a long time.

I found out from staff that the doctor who upset me was hired by Wakenhut [private corporation contracted to run prisons] specifically to cut psychotropic drugs. On June 4th he discontinued my antidepressants. He said that they don't like to leave people on them forever. So even though I told him how scared I was because I had never been without them since everything had happened, he stopped them. The first few weeks were okay, but the last three weeks have been hell. I've felt so out of control emotionally. I've been agitated easily, my anxiety level is high. I'm either mad or crying. Finally, I lost it, crying hysterically and furious because I've tried for six months to get therapy and everyone tells me they'll take care of it but do nothing. (Christina)

Before the priest reappeared in my life I had applied for a summer job at a camp for the blind in Pennsylvania. Just when the pain and confusion of "therapy" seemed unsurvivable, I received word I'd been hired.

A woman I'd grown up with, whose mother lived across the street from mine, was in the middle of her own crisis. She wanted to go to Pennsylvania to try and locate her five children, kidnapped by her husband and another woman one day while she was at work. I decided to accept the summer job, so we drove together. The day I left I wrote a letter to the psychiatrist and told him I wouldn't be in. I decided if they wanted to track me down they could.

Sometimes I just want to give up but I keep thinking of other people who may find themselves in the same position, and perhaps I can make a difference. That's why I keep fighting. (Debra)

The two of us set out across country. She knew nothing of the problems I had. We'd be driving along and her eyes would fill up with tears. I'd look over, see them streaming down her cheeks, and I'd start to cry, too. She always thought I was crying for her.

Each day we'd stop somewhere for an hour or so to rest. We rested apart, but sometimes I could see her from my spot. She'd take out the cracked and worn pictures of her husband and children, look at them, and quietly weep. I'd write long letters to Beth, letters I'd never mail and she'd never see, letters that helped me survive.

You cannot write to people who do not want to hear from you. I've never had that happen, but it's in cases such as an inmate trying to intimidate a witness in their case, or an old boyfriend. That type of thing. The inmate is then put on a restricted mailing list. (Robin)

As we traveled I made myself come to grips with the idea of going to prison. I was convinced that if they came after me, I surely would. I felt protected as long as we were in the car driving because no one knew where I was. But I also realized that freedom could be taken from me at any moment. So I made myself sit quietly each day and visualize being in prison. After I had grown used to that, after I got over the fright, it didn't bother me as much. And it wasn't too difficult to imagine because inside myself I was already there.

The prison here just opened in January 1997. It can hold six hundred females and it always stays full. They plan to build an extra two hundred beds by spring. Death row consists of the Segregation/Discipline Unit. I have my own shower and outside rec area. I'm allowed two hours/six days a week for recreation outside. So unless I'm at recreation, visits, showering, or using the phone, I'm in my cell. (Christina)

Things went smoothly at the camp, better than I'd imagined. I'd never known anyone with a physical or mental handicap. That's one reason I'd applied to work at a camp for the blind. I needed to learn more about how others lived. During our pre-camp instructions I was told that the people in the first session would be from state mental hospitals. In addition to being blind, they were also retarded, brain damaged, and psychotic, suffering from a variety of mental disorders. I had no preconceived notions about what that all meant.

The camp was hidden in the Appalachian mountains on the banks of the Juniata, a broad, lazy river. Thick fog would hover over the water in the early mornings, and sometimes in the predawn hours I'd stand there and wait for it to come around the wide bend and let a part of me move along with it. I started breathing on my own again.

I am allowed fresh air for one hour, four times a week, but sometimes I don't come out of my cell or talk to people for weeks. I've gotten used to being locked inside and mostly like to keep to myself. There are mice running around and there are two owls right outside my window that eat them. It's amazing how God balances things out. (Andrea)

4.

I took the money I'd made that summer and enrolled at a Michigan university in bilingual education. It was there that I saw a notice in the student union about a lesbian gathering. I wanted to go. Of course I hadn't forgotten the words from Beth's aunt. I may have been indistinguishable from "all of those homos," but I was still curious about who they were and what they *really* looked like. I attended the meeting and found women who reminded me of the women I'd lived with all my life. Women I liked. I started going to the meetings on a regular basis.

I just feel more comfortable in relationships with women. Women always turned me on more than men and I have felt this way since I was a little girl. And I've been married to three different men. But I've lived with women and had a number of relationships with them, too. Basically women were always there for me during the bad times. Even in here. (Carolyn)

Another year went by. It felt good to be moving toward something, to be restructuring my life. I returned to the camp for the blind in the summer. This time I was hired as director of the adult unit. It was a big job, but one that I wanted. I needed to feel productive and worthy, to succeed. I was still plagued with thoughts of what I'd done. I couldn't forgive myself.

Two days before the camp opened I was summoned on the phone by the camp's director. He didn't sound like himself, and the pit of my stomach reacted. Because he was blind he couldn't see the fear my eyes might have betrayed when I went to his office. He handed me a typewritten letter telling me I had forty-eight hours to vacate the premises. It did not say why. Beth's mother had struck again.

The director apologized. He said he no longer believed I was suitable for the job, that the camp had the right to cancel my contract, and that he was doing so. Then he offered me a one-way ticket to anywhere. There would be no questions or requests for explanations. Like the others, he didn't want to know. When asked to leave the orientation program I had so carefully prepared, I said no.

It was only the intervention of all twenty-six counselors, who told the director that they would resign if he didn't re-hire me, that enabled me to keep my job. There wasn't time to hire a new staff, so he came to see me and asked me to stay. I did, but it wasn't the same. Something had gone out of me.

In my years on death row I have already had the horrible experience of being served with two death warrants. My death warrant was signed twice and I received two stays, but they refused to move me out of the Phase 2 room or allow me regular showers when I was in Phase 2. When I received my stays I was left in the Phase 2 room for seven and

a half months before they moved me, which is cruel and un-
usual punishment and mental torture.

I am trying to find someone who will help me get DNA
testing done because I believe this is the only way that my
innocence will be proven. Although I have requested this of
the public defenders representing me, my request is still be-
ing ignored and denied. I'm sure the third time, if I just sit
here and do nothing about it, will cost me my life for sure.
(Donetta)

Two years had passed since Beth. I finished my studies
and applied for teaching positions throughout the country.
Although my records stated I had resigned for personal reasons, Beth's mother had threatened she'd see to it I never
taught again. While I didn't completely believe her, she had
certainly already caused me difficulties. I had no references
that would stand up to hard scrutiny, and it did not occur to
me to invent them. I wrote letters about where I'd been and
what I'd done in my teaching career, conveniently leaving
out the year that revolved around Beth. I hoped people
would be impressed. One school was.

It was a girl's boarding school in Maryland. They called
while I was still at camp. Would I come for an interview? I
was ecstatic. I was hired as the head of the foreign language
department and was assigned the job of overseeing the soph-
omore dorm. The girls were wonderful. They were wild and
alive and I loved them. I received positive feedback on my
work and was proud to feel healthy and whole again.

When I returned after spending the Christmas holidays
with my mother, however, I knew something was wrong. At
Sunday dinner that first night back I felt a knot in the pit of
my stomach. It wasn't anything anyone said. It may have
been a look, or the long silences that hung in the air between
each sentence I spoke. Whatever had transpired, I sensed

that somebody, maybe everybody, knew. I went to bed with a heavy heart waiting for the axe to fall.

It appears that in Pennsylvania the system is telling us if you are a woman sentenced to death, you are no longer women but caged animals (for twenty-three hours a day, five days a week, and for twenty-four hours a day the other two). And you have no right to try and feel like a woman. I can only speak for myself, but I think that when the judge sentenced me to death he did not put a clause in stating that SCI-Muncy has the right or responsibility to punish me again and again and again until the day I die. (Carolyn)

During my second-period Spanish class the next morning, another teacher came and told me I was needed in the office. The principal was sitting behind her desk when I entered, a tape recorder and two pieces of paper in front of her. A graying fortyish man sat across the room. He shifted uncomfortably, I thought, as I walked in.

I knew what was about to happen. The principal said the man was a psychiatrist. She said he was there to mediate. She said our conversation would be recorded. I felt a familiar numbness spread over me. I'd been there before. I knew the players and all the moves.

She'd learned of my past, she said. I'd been under psychiatric care and run away. The recorder swished. I had two options. There were always two. I could resign my position immediately, or stay until the end of the year and see this psychiatrist on a weekly basis. To leave would be to let control slip away again. I stayed.

When the deputy warden read the death warrant to me, although I knew it was coming, I felt like I had been kicked in the stomach. The deputy warden was having a difficult time reading it. After he had finished, we sat quietly for a few minutes. In the room was myself, the deputy warden, and Carol, the counselor. The deputy warden said I wouldn't have to worry as I would get a stay when I went to the federal courts. The look of shock on his face was hard to deal with when I told him I wasn't appealing. He asked me to give it some thought. He felt I should go on to the federal courts. That I could change my mind then, but to give myself a chance. (Robin)

The rules were the same: no discussions with anyone. If I missed appointments, I'd be subject to immediate termination of my employment. I couldn't be alone with a student. No students could come into my bedroom. I was not allowed in any dorm except the one I lived in. Another dorm advisor would move in next to me.

The psychiatrist's office was two miles from the school. I walked there twice a week. I kicked stones all the way. He asked me what girls in the school I fantasized about and what parts of their bodies turned me on. His talk made me sick. I was nearly crazy again.

The reality is it was a long walk to isolation. If the officers weren't holding on to my elbows, I would have fallen many times. I kept tripping on the coveralls. As I walked, each step led me closer to a place that would be my "home" for years to come. Until the authorities felt it was my time to die.

Then these same officers watched me take a shower in handcuffs. Can you imagine showering in handcuffs? It's not easy. An officer poured lice shampoo all over my hair. I was so upset that I started shaking. I was given white coveralls that were grayer than white to put on, with no underclothes. The coveralls were several inches too long and several sizes too big. I was given a pair of men's shower shoes, size ten. I wore a women's six. I had trouble keeping them on my feet. Once I was dressed they put leg irons and belly chains on me and removed the handcuffs. Trying to dress with them was a real challenge. (Robin)

I went to the principal and told her I couldn't stand the pressure of seeing this man twice a week. I wanted her to tell me what I'd done, there, in that school, that had made this necessary. I knew my behavior had been impeccable. She said there was always potential.

They used to handcuff and shackle me for my three-hour visits with my mom. Even though I was locked in a room by myself, with glass between us. Just a few weeks ago I left the prison to go the doctor in town and they locked down the whole compound till I was out of the building. They had three officers escort me out. I know they were just following policy but I thought, I've never given them any trouble. In fact, although most of the officers call me a model inmate, I'm listed as an "assault risk" because I'm on death row. (Christina)

I told the psychiatrist I was in pain. He offered no help. Then one day he asked if I'd ever fantasized about him. Suddenly, I understood his game. So I told him yes and described in great detail the size I imagined his penis to be. And I watched him squirm contentedly as he put a book over his lap. I almost threw up. But then he offered help. He wrote me a prescription for Valium and life became bearable. I told him stories; he let me have as much Valium as I wanted. I ate it like candy.

I want off this psychiatric medication I am taking, but

my psychiatrist says if I stop taking it I will have a relapse and it will be very difficult for me to recuperate. Right now I am taking thirty milligrams of Prozac and thirty milligrams of Sinecuan in the morning, and thirty milligrams of Sinecuan at night. (Ana)

I took a summer job working in an Upward Bound program. There I learned I was addicted. With no pharmacist to run to when my bottle of Valium was empty, the supply quickly dried up. I went into withdrawal about twenty-four hours after my last pill. I was deathly sick and didn't know what was wrong. I was clammy and trembling with dry heaves. It felt like my insides were being ripped apart. I thought I was going to die.

The doctor who was called asked if I took drugs. I said no. Drugs were what you bought on the street; I was on medication. But his question clued me in. For three days I fought the terror and pain, and then it subsided. I was exhausted but still alive. I knew I would go on.

Part 3

Matins

A
canonical
hour
of
psalms
of
joy
recited
at
dawn

1.

In the end, it was my mother who found a way to explain what was happening in my life. For reasons that remained forever hers, in the summer of 1978 she started telling people who asked her about me that I was a "sister-at-large." The first time I heard her say this was in a telephone conversation with my cousin Shirley, who must have asked her why I was home again and what I was doing. Mother was sitting in the dining room, close to the large curtained windows, the heat of a Kansas July pouring off her brow. In her hand she gripped the heavy black telephone we'd had since I was a child.

I was in the living room on the old red divan, still coping with the aftereffects of Valium withdrawal and trying, once again, to learn to breathe on my own. I liked the way *sister-at-large* sounded. My mother, in her own strange way, had come through for me, and I was grateful. Having a term for who I was gave me a sense of identity and security. We never discussed how she came up with this title, or whether or not it was true. The simple fact that my mother said it made it so.

I think about holing up in my mom's apartment a lot, and about the two of us eating good food and talking for hours and hours. I think about sleeping in a comfortable bed, taking a shower in a clean shower, and drinking lots of juice—real 100 percent juice. I think about a lot of things like that, but mostly about how much family means. (Debra)

It could have been the culture of silence I grew up in, or the support I'd received from the Catholic Church in maintaining it, but the truth of the matter was that even though I'd been told to leave the convent, I didn't have a clue about how to do it. And since it was not my idea in the first place, I felt little or no motivation to find out.

The first community I belonged to may have thought the community I was transferring to had told me what to do, and the community I thought I'd transferred to may have felt it was the duty of my original community to inform me, but in what now seems to have been a religious loophole of sorts, no one said anything to me other than I should leave.

I had taken final vows and, in the eyes of the Catholic Church, at least technically I was still a nun. Regardless of what had occurred.

Me and my husband were both found guilty and sentenced to death at the trial. I was sentenced first, but it didn't fully impact me at the time because I was focusing on my husband. So when the judge asked me if I had anything to say after he read my sentence, I said no. When my husband's death sentence was read and the judge asked him if he had anything to say, he got up in the courtroom and tearfully told everyone how sorry he was. While I was listening to him I kept waiting for him to say, But your honor, my wife had nothing to do with this. Of course, he never did say that, and since that moment my life has been a nightmare. (Kelley)

That was a very shaky summer for me. I was fighting depression most of the time. Being in such close proximity to the community that had asked me to leave, as well as being well-known in the town where I'd grown up, was extremely difficult. I spent a lot of time sitting on the couch, concentrating on my next breath.

I've been having a hard time since I got out from under that first death warrant. They've kept me in the mental health unit, and the doctor is trying to send me through detox because I became addicted to the medicine I was on. She want-

ed me to gain pounds so I could be healthy enough to be ex-
ecuted. I'm on Ensure and vitamins for the weight gain. I
don't know if they're helping or not. She didn't want to re-
lease me, but I signed myself out against her will. (Carolyn)

My mother spent her time doing what seemed to me like interminable odd jobs in the kitchen and dining room, while I stayed in my bedroom or the living room. We both had our territory and managed to move in and around each other quite well. Some evenings we sat and watched TV together. We rarely spoke.

Mother always cooked meals, and we ate sitting across from each other in the breakfast nook my father had proudly built when I was nine or ten. Though I had no appetite, I felt obligated to sit with her at least twice a day. She asked me once, during a meal, if I was okay, telling me that she thought I looked sad. This brought tears to my eyes, but I told her I was fine and she did not ask again.

In the Restricted Housing Unit, we are subjected to con-
stant verbal abuse by staff as well as from other inmates
who call us "death row bitches." "Are you scared to die?"
they say. Or, when I once asked an officer for a light, he said,
"They'll give you one last one before they fry you." (Kelley)

I thought about the days of turmoil after Beth when I traveled by Greyhound bus and there were long delays in dirty little depots between changes. I was usually feeling lonely, and often only in the company of the seedy-looking characters who seemed to proliferate in those kind of places. I'd been propositioned more than once and, perhaps out of fear rather than desperation, I took to pretending I had people to call.

I used to live for my mail and telephone calls. When I first came to prison I received a lot of mail, but as time goes by people get busy with their lives and I fade into the background. I don't call many people because nothing changes in my life, so what do I have to talk about. It's also depressing for them. (Robin)

It was in the pages of Ma-Bell phone books that I found a gold mine. Many cities had numbers listed under *Dial* that you could call and get a recording giving you information on almost anything. There were things like Dial-a-Prayer, Dial-a-Recipe, Dial-an-Artist, Dial-the-Weather, and once, perhaps in Memphis, I found Dial Elvis. This was a recorded message from the King himself about the birth of his daughter.

I called these numbers whenever I felt threatened and would just stand and listen to the voice at the other end. I did this for several years, even beyond my immediate need for it. If a message was particularly soothing or otherwise appealing, I might listen to it twice. But Salina, Kansas, had no such numbers, and there were days that summer when I was consumed by loneliness.

I sometimes ask myself why I should go on like this— suffering and crying every day. I would rather put an end to it. Today has been a day when I have no desire to live. Loneliness is bad and one thinks about suicide. I say this because I feel that way. I have a difficult time feeling I am alive. (Ana)

I'd gone back to my routines in order to help me survive: counting my way through daily activities and adhering to a schedule. Mass in the morning followed by breakfast, then three or four hours at the library. Home to check in and off to the park on my bike to write. Even though several years had passed, I felt dangerously close to falling again. Where exactly, I didn't know.

I spend most of my time reading, sleeping, and exercising in my cell. I used to try to get together with the other women to protest prison conditions or to try to get the same privileges death row men have. The men have jobs, they get showers every day, and they have pajamas and bathrobes and slippers. Men get together on these things, but us women barely have enough strength to get up each day. Some of us don't even do that. (Kelley)

And then the nightmares began. Frequently, in the middle of the night, my heart racing, soaked in sweat, I'd waken myself screaming. At other times I'd feel my mother, small and frail, bending over me, shaking me into sensibility when I was unable to climb out of the pit myself.

One night I had a dream of being in a large cathedral filled with people I didn't know. I was sitting in a pew in the center. People were coming in and squeezing themselves into the overflowing benches on either end so that I was being pressed tightly on both sides. Touching arms and elbows with strangers.

The church was ornate. It could have been St. Patrick's in New York City. Before the services started, I became aware of two men behind me who were talking about me. I couldn't determine what it was they were saying. I didn't know either of them, but it didn't feel good. It seemed like they might have been judging me, though for what I couldn't say.

Please tell everyone that the one thing I'd like is to have "Forever Young" played at my execution. I don't know if you know this song. It's by Rod Stewart. I'll sing it for you. (Kelley)

The dream was filled with anxiety. The services ended as quickly as they began, and everyone rose to leave. The crowd inched slowly toward large wooden doors. We were packed tightly, moving as one. A huge human amoeba, of sorts. At the entrance, I saw the street for the first time. It was a field of pits—they seemed bottomless—looking much like a furnace filter. The sight terrified me and I froze. No one else seemed aware of any danger as the crowd spilled out around me into the street.

It was hard to believe people didn't care about the horrendous mouths yawning at their feet, as if they knew they were there and had somehow learned to manipulate them. There was no hesitation, but much laughing and talking as individuals and groups showed amazing dexterity walking around on the small spaces between the holes without looking down at their feet.

I ran back to the cavernous nave of the church in panic, first to the front, then to the sides, seeking another way out. There was none, and I awoke screaming.

At one point I began to hallucinate about a noose hanging in front of me. I often wondered whether or not it was really there—and if it wasn't there, how could I put one there. (Andrea)

I was sitting on the couch facing the front door as usual, one afternoon, when a police car pulled up to the curb and stopped. I went numb. Two uniformed officers got out and came up the front walk. I met them at the door. The old mesh screen between us offered little protection. My mother was taking a nap, and I was convinced she'd awaken to find me gone. Some neighbor would later inform her they'd seen me leave handcuffed to one of these representatives of the law.

I started out in a boat with a small hole in it, but the hole kept getting bigger. No matter how hard I tried to bail, I kept sinking. Finally, I was tired and gave up. (Christina)

The three of us looked at each other. The officers were calm and smiling. It was a bit unnerving: I couldn't imagine they'd be so pleasant about coming to arrest anyone. Especially a nun. When one of them put his hand close to his holster and tucked his fingers in his belt, I was sure they were there for me. Then the taller one spoke and asked me in a deep courteous voice if I was interested in buying a ticket for the circus the Salina police department was sponsoring for the local children's hospital. I politely declined, and as I watched them leave, I steadied myself on the door. It was several minutes before my heart stopped pounding.

Sick call is conducted at your cell door. If a referral is made to see a doctor there is no guarantee that will happen. There may not be any cars available or they can just cancel it without telling you why. (Carolyn)

2.

As the summer progressed I came to the realization I probably would not be able to teach high school again. I felt that what had happened with Beth would pursue me wherever I went and that I didn't want to continue living in fear and pain. Accepting and making peace with this personal demon was both difficult and deeply disappointing. I was a good teacher, and I loved being part of the learning process, but I recognized it was time to consider other options. What else could I do?

There were two things I knew. The first one was that I

wanted to live in community. The second was that I could work with handicapped people. It didn't occur to me at the time that there might be a way to combine the two.

The things I liked to do the most on the outside were cooking, cleaning, and taking care of my kids. I particularly loved to clean. Now I get a bucket of disinfectant to clean my cell three times a week, but I have to use the same rag for months. I wash my cell floor with shampoo. When I lay on my bunk at night, I put the covers over my head so I don't see the dirt I can't reach. It's like laying in your own casket, which is good preparation for the future in here. (Kelley)

The issue of community had already begun to resolve itself. I first learned about the Sisters for Christian Community (SFCC) after my involvement with Beth became known. Two members of the order taught at the same high school. When they heard I was leaving they encouraged me to consider joining them. SFCC began as a small group of women who had left other religious communities but did not wish to leave religious life altogether. With this in mind they had started their own order, a noncanonical order removed from the pope's jurisdiction. The name the first members chose reflected the group's vision: they wanted to be *sisters* first, with the intent of creating Christian community.

The fear, the restrictions, the long lonely hours, the taunting, and the lack of a real life is what makes day-to-day living so painful. (Robin)

You could join SFCC by simply signing up. If you had vows in another order, you kept them. Members lived on their own and supported themselves, unless they chose to live in groups, which was also permitted. The actual running of the community, which at the time meant answering letters, sending out a newsletter, and advising members of upcoming events, was handled by rotation. There was no motherhouse and no convents. Every two years the people who did the paperwork changed so that the community address was wherever the people who were answering the mail lived.

No one seemed interested in why you wanted to leave one order and join another, nor in how long you might want to stay. Nuns who lived in the same state tried to get together once a month for a day of prayer and socializing. There was an annual community meeting each summer.

Joining SFCC was a great relief for me. It meant, among other things, that I was still a nun and that there was a name to indicate where I belonged. I didn't have to sever my religious ties completely.

Now that the spiritual part of my life seemed taken care of, I had to look for a job.

It's very hard to live day after day and not know what to do. When you see what I see and feel what I feel, there's no way out. My sorrow and loneliness are huge. To be forgotten is the worst. (Ana)

Although I was doing better emotionally, my nightmares continued. I couldn't earn enough to live on from the intermittent substitute teaching I had managed to secure both at a public and the Catholic high school. Since my previous experience at the camp for the blind had been so rich, I began to look for work with handicapped people. I would often draw on the strength of those days. I'd learned the beauty of the present moment, the importance of living and enjoying the now. The special adults I'd known didn't care who I'd been or what I'd done. They accepted me for who I was.

Some people will find out about me and say this is what I deserve. That, after all, I'm on death row. But I think this kind of treatment is wrong. I believe only God can be the judge. Losing your freedom is the punishment, being locked up and away from society. But nowhere does it say that an inmate has to be treated like a wild animal. (Robin)

In one of my many searches at the Salina Public Library I came across a write-up about a place in Virginia called Innisfree Village. I loved the name and the fact that the word *free* was part of it. I felt called to it. In fact, I had a similar reaction to the one I experienced in high school when the book about religious communities fell off the shelf at my feet.

3.

When I arrived at Innisfree in May of 1979 I didn't know that it had been someone's dream; I only knew it was my hope.

Nine years before I got there a group of parents of mentally handicapped adults had shared concerns about the future of their children. Innisfree was born out of these discussions, conceived as a life-span facility where adults with various mental disabilities—including retardation, emotional disturbances, autism, and brain trauma—would live in community with each other and staff members. There would be no therapies except community life itself. It was and continues to be an alternative to institutionalization.

I remember my son's birth. Chris brought me so much joy I can't even describe it. He did everything early and learned things quickly. I had a rocking chair and I'd just hold him and rock him all the time. Then when he got older, as a tod-

dler, he liked George Strait. He'd ask me to play some George Strait, and when I'd put it on the stereo I'd dance with him and pick him up and whirl him around the room. He liked it most when I'd just hold him close and very slowly sway. (Debra)

To accomplish their dream, the parents formed a nonprofit organization and bought 550 acres at the foot of the Shenandoah National Park in the Blue Ridge Mountains. Walnut Level was the only house on the property when it was purchased. Built in the 1700s in a grove of walnut trees, it retains much of its original strength and splendor today.

Eight houses and several other buildings—including barns, a community center, and a gymnasium—now make up the village where some thirty-five mentally handicapped adults and thirty staff live together in family.

I dream of being with my children again. For this reason I am happy that there are people working to abolish the death penalty. What anti-death penalty groups do is a labor of love. (Ana)

After my application was accepted, I agreed to stay at Innisfree for one year. It was a safety measure for me, something I was gradually learning: don't move too fast. A year at a time seemed like all I could handle. On the application I had indicated I was a nun. They wrote back emphasizing that Innisfree was a secular community:

> Our philosophy and approach embrace a humanistic focus and that is our unifying principle. There are some at Innisfree who are mildly religious, and others not at all. Some are Unitarian, Jewish, Hindu, Agnostic, nonbelievers, and Chris-

tians. Each is accepted for his/her belief. And I must say, in all honesty, that I am much relieved that you do not feel called to stand on a mountaintop to preach, as we do not actively seek conversion for anyone here.

This was good. I arose, as the William Butler Yeats poem encouraged, and went to Innisfree. I didn't build myself a cabin, but I did find some peace there. I never spoke about being a nun, and blending in was not difficult. I knew how to do that. In many ways, Innisfree was the easiest and most nourishing community I'd ever lived in. In some of the lessons it taught me, it was not. One of the first was that I no longer needed a title. Beginning a new life, I regained my own name: I was no longer Sister. Forever after, I was Kathy O'Shea.

The media continues to refer to me as Lynda Lyon Block. My name is Lyon not Block. It ceased being Block after my divorce decree restored my birth name. The fact that my true name appeared on the indictment, but not on the actual court papers, proves the Alabama state bar association courts knew that Block has not been part of my name since 1992, but they continue to issue papers in this fictitious name, to make it appear as if George and I are not married. (Lynda)

Disabled is an unfortunate word we've become accustomed to using for "differently gifted" people. An early Innisfree lesson was the realization that we humans are all differently gifted. The people we apply the term *disabled* to are those who, for whatever reason, we recognize by what they cannot do rather than by what they can.

Amidst the give and take of community life, Innisfree

oozed peace, acceptance, joy, and idealism. We lived in family groups in houses with names like Meadow (my house), Sunflower, Dogwood, and Halcyon. We went to work each day at the weavery, the bakery, the woodshop, or the garden. There were three work periods daily, and people could change where they worked each period. In the evenings we returned to our homes and did what families do—we just lived.

I've never felt so much anger and loneliness. I feel totally helpless to do anything about what people say or do to me in here. It's what the whole thing is about—degrading you as much as possible. (Carolyn)

Then I met Monica. It snowed till March that year. With fresh bread from the bakery and milk from the cows, I set out across the fields to find her. I'd seen her drive up the mountain in her black VW bug and disappear almost every day, but we'd never met. People said she lived alone in the huge old house she rented for twenty-five dollars a month in exchange for tending the land. With four days of storms threatening to blanket the fences, I thought she might not have food. And I needed to get out of the house.

She stood there, a miracle in the midst of my loneliness, looking lonely too. *Thanks* was all Monica said. I danced all the way back to Meadow making angels in fields of virgin snow.

I don't want to talk about my suffering, but I have to tell someone in order to get rid of it. I feel desperate and helpless. The only thing I can do is cry. (Ana)

She lived at Turkey Ridge. The dilapidated castle of our kingdom of love. It was a rickety old house where nothing was right except the time we shared there. In the winter she occupied a single room downstairs, the one with the wood-burning stove. And when the wind whipped down the mountains at night, we were almost certain the house would fall. We made love for the first time in a huge old bed under an ancient quilt that had been covering a hole in the wall. Afterward she prayed to Sai Baba, the East Indian spiritual leader, and I lay very still. We'd both been alone for so long.

You can't imagine what I went through with my woman friend. She beat me bloody and forced me to have sex with her. In many ways I was destroyed both morally and physically. Now I live in constant fear. She hurt me terribly by taking away what I loved the most, my children. (Ana)

Monica was sweet and gentle, we were both afraid. Nakedness teaching trust. She glowed prettier than anyone I'd ever seen. Each time we met I wanted to stay and keep her glowing forever. At sunrise I'd pull myself away and race over the fields to slip through the fence and be home before anyone else was up. This was the first winter it was spring in my heart. A quiet peace settled in my soul.

She'd wake me up at three or four in the morning and if I refused to have sex with her she'd wake the children up and drive us all out to some deserted place and leave us there. My daughter was four years old, and my sons were two and nine. And just before she'd drive off she'd remind me that when I was ready to do what was expected of me she'd come back and get us. (Ana)

She showed me a road through a river and said that a woman lived at the top of the ridge. She didn't like to talk that much. "Liza's place," she'd say. Then she explained how she could drive her car down the riverbed until it ran into the road that led to Liza's door. It was such a hidden place.

We'd go there sometimes and bathe in the middle of the stream in broad daylight. I'd sit on a log and dangle my feet in the water, feeling the cleansing coolness cover my toes. I'd let myself drift with the clouds. We'd hold each other without words until the sun began to set. Then, reluctantly, we'd wade through the stream to her car on the other side.

I'd beg her not to leave us. The children would be crying and I'd plead with her to take them back to the house. I'd even get on my knees and beg her. She'd tell me it was my decision. Finally, I'd say, Do whatever you want with me, but have pity on my children. Then she'd leave us and return in two or three hours. (Ana)

Monica pumped water from the well to bathe. Sometimes, when it was icy, we'd stand in the sun and pour it over each other—baptisms of love. I'd spread the water on her shoulders, her breasts, her belly, and she'd stand there glowing. A receptive canvas, a masterpiece. Never self-conscious. My living madonna. Her body would tremble when a breeze caught us off guard.

I cried bitterly. I couldn't have sex with her. She did a lot of terrible things to me, but there didn't seem to be a way out. So I took drugs—cocaine. I thought I needed it. It took me to another world, a world where everything was dark and I couldn't feel anything. That way I could let her do whatever she wanted with me. She would have sex with me when I was stoned until she had had enough. I would keep my eyes closed and the tears would run. (Ana)

On Wednesday mornings before the village awoke we'd meditate. I'd walk from Meadow, up past Halcyon, all the way to the barn between our properties. Then I'd sit and wait on a rock. She usually appeared with Champ, her mixed mutt, at her heels, and the three of us would go to the high pasture. She'd sing to Sai Babba and anoint me from head to toe with ashes from her pilgrimage.

I think that a relationship between two women should be sweet, something sublime, with love and passion. The flame of fire that makes you vibrate. I regret I've never known this kind of love. My life has been hard and destiny has treated me cruelly. (Ana)

Life at Innisfree went on. I worked in the bakery in the morning and the garden in the afternoon. I loved kneading and weeding. There was a rhythmic monotony to both of those activities that helped bring order to my life.

It was a hot, muggy summer, and we baled hay several times. A telephone call alerted us when we were supposed to go out to the fields. The two main jobs in baling were either picking up the sixty-pound bales and heaving them onto the wagon, or stacking them on the wagon. Tossing was, by far, the easier job. If you misstacked even one bale, the whole wagonload might topple and you had to start over.

The appeals court ordered us to be taken back to the trial judge for a hearing to determine whether we were mentally capable. This was after George and I refused to let any lawyers handle our case. We weren't going to play their games. So when the judge tried to question us about our education and experience we refused to give any information. We only told him he had no legal standing to force us to participate in his charade. After that day, the judges never forced us back to court again. (Lynda)

In September, after fifteen months, I returned to Salina to teach English and Spanish full-time at the Catholic high school. I was at home at Innisfree, but an offer to teach was hard for me to turn down. Being able to go back to the classroom felt like such a victory.

The new principal at Sacred Heart was a man I'd met while substitute teaching. One day, before classes began, he called me into his office and told me he'd heard everything there was to hear about me and that it made no difference to him. Like a host of others, he never told me what he'd heard, and I never asked. He did say that he knew I could teach, and that that was the only thing of interest to him. It took barely three months for me to figure out that I loved the teaching but my heart was somewhere else. I wrote and told the Innisfree community I wanted to return at the end of the school year.

If an officer doesn't like you, he/she can make your life miserable. I happen to have an officer who doesn't like me. I hear you say, What can be harder than death row? Well, let me tell you. This officer will call me at six in the morning to take a shower, and if I want a shower that day it is then or not at all. I am allowed to shower for fifteen minutes, and if I go one minute over, believe me he will give me a warning slip. When I get out of the shower, he doesn't give me time to get dressed before he calls me to take my one hour a day recreation time. If it is warm out, that's not a problem, but I won't go out in cold weather with my hair wet. At those times, I refuse. Too many of those days, though, and I'll go out anyway because I have cabin fever.

My meals will come, and he will let them sit there. This causes the food to get cold. My ice cream has melted, my gravy congeals, pasta will stick together. My mail comes at four but he will wait and give it to me at nine, even when he isn't busy. If I have a telephone call scheduled at seven, he won't let me make it until eight or nine. Not that the phone is busy—I'm the only one here. He will withhold my supplies and search my room more than once in a shift. Oh yes, life can be made much worse. (Robin)

4.

Another year passed at Innisfree. Then I received an invitation to submit the story of what had happened to me—*my story*—to the editors of a proposed book about lesbian nuns:

> Please share your stories of convent life, coming out as a lesbian, struggles to transform your spiritual consciousness, and anything else for a collection to be published by Naiad Press.

I sat down on my day off and wrote for almost twelve uninterrupted hours. Apparently the story had been in me long enough. Once I started putting it down on paper, the words gushed. I filled up two and a half legal pads. When the words stopped coming, it felt as if an enormous weight had been lifted. I typed the story up and called it "No Place Left to Hide," then sent copies to the two editors.

I know my case isn't on the books yet. I once asked my attorneys about the trial transcript and was told that that alone was over forty-five hundred pages. If you add all the pretrial hearings and the sentencing hearing and the actual sentencing, we are talking about ten thousand additional pages of transcript. (Robin)

In time, I heard from both the editors. One said that what I wrote was "powerful, painful, enlightening," and reaffirmed her resolve to do the book. She said stories like mine should be heard, that they are empowering to all women. The other said she could hardly breathe the whole time she was reading it. Even though she thought my story was too long, she encouraged me to write more. They each confided that reading my story had moved them to write their own.

The editors assured me that they intended to edit the book in the most caring and feminist way they knew. My story was soon in its third draft, the result of many back-and-forth interchanges by mail. The piece was shaping up.

One thing you never adjust to is the lack of privacy. This is one of the hardest things. They check through the peephole every hour, or anytime they want. You think you're sitting there alone and in private, but this isn't always the case. And we're talking about men guards, too. I'm not supposed to, but when I use the bathroom I put a piece of paper over the window of my cell. (Andrea)

At Innisfree, I had found my cloister. I loved the community process. The challenge of different people coming together for a common purpose was an atmosphere in which I thrived. By the time the lesbian nun book was developed, I'd been there for almost three years. Paradoxically, the love and acceptance I experienced at Innisfree freed me to look beyond its boundaries and dream of other ways of living. So when one of the editors asked me if I'd like to help put the book together, I was more than eager. I decided to try and arrange a leave of absence for a few months. I would help type and edit, and then return.

This is the seventh birthday I've spent on death row. I

dream of being with my daughters again. I don't know if I can fight another three years because my soul and mind are already tired and run down. I hate when my birthday rolls around each year because it is supposed to be a special day. But for me, it's just another day in hell. The question I ask myself is: Do I want to live another year in hell, or do I want to die to escape this living hell? (Donetta)

The writer in me was attracted to the possibility of working on a book. I'd never done anything like it before. When I presented the idea of a sabbatical to the Innisfree community, they were open to it—if I could wait until the summer. I understood their position, but I didn't have flexibility. The manuscript had to be finished by the summer, and I had already agreed to have the editors send me copies of stories to read and comment on.

When I couldn't get the community to agree to an immediate leave of absence, I decided to forget the idea of a sabbatical and just leave. I was, for better or worse, well-schooled in the art of expeditious departures.

I think about my children a lot. I've never really been able to grieve. I was not able to say good-bye to them. People who know me say that although a part of me recognized what had happened, another part was in denial. Without realizing it, I sometimes speak about my children in the present tense. Although they've been gone for over five years, it's still difficult to talk about. Sometimes it feels like it just happened yesterday. The pain is so great. (Robin)

Despite the editors' assurances, they had apparently begun to have doubts about my story early on. They sent copies of the stories that were chosen for the collection to four outside readers. At least two of them objected to mine.

They felt my story was a case of child abuse. They said that to allow my story in the book along with the others was to condone what they felt I had done. One of those readers had suffered abuse as a child herself.

When these readers' objections were voiced, words like *morality, sinfulness, criminality, legality,* and *power dynamics* were all spoken in the same sentence with my name. The editors suggested I rewrite the story more as an examination of conscience. That I include answers to questions such as: *Why did I think I did what I did? Did I regret it? Did I consider my holy vows while I was doing it?*

For six and one-half years I have been telling EVERYBODY that I'm innocent, but no one wants to listen, nor do they care. The media have a horrible name for me—which is murderer. And which is all anyone knows me as. But God knows they are wrong. (Donetta)

It had not occurred to me that with publication, my life might once again not be my own, that I could be on the run. And so I made the decision to take my story out of *Lesbian Nuns* barely before the book went to press.

I disagree with a lot with what the professionals write. Some of it is so obviously wrong. At one time I was focused on setting the record straight, but no one would listen to me or change their views, so I gave up. (Ana)

I got a job working at a school for mentally handicapped adults a few blocks from my new apartment. This was the first time I'd lived alone. I had one bedroom, with a living room, kitchen, and a bathroom. The apartment was unfurnished, so I slept on the floor and stacked my things in the closet until after my first paycheck. I rented a bed, a couch, and a lamp. I also bought a secondhand bike which I rode to school. Despite everything, I was feeling good. I had done something positive to move my life forward.

On the inside I've had to fight for everything I have. People keep saying prisons are so easy. If you're out in the yard on Thursday, for example, and it's summer and you get hot and sweaty, you can't take a shower until Monday. No showers on Friday, Saturday, Sunday. So I've learned to bathe in my sink. But can you imagine how hard it is to fit this big old body into a sink? (Andrea)

5.

Amy came to interview for a job at the school where I worked. I probably wouldn't have noticed her if she hadn't been placed in my classroom to observe for a week. There were ten profoundly retarded adults and two aides and Amy. She rarely said anything. She just watched what I did all day. Then she was hired. I learned she'd recently married when she brought wedding pictures to show in the teachers' lounge.

I thought it was all right at first when she started dropping by my apartment, although it was not something I initiated. I was happy seeing people during the day and being home in my own space at night. Before her, no one came and no one called and I liked that.

I didn't know how to tell her to go away and stay away. I hated rejection myself and couldn't inflict it on her. I did wonder, though, what her new husband might be doing without her. Her visits got longer, and she started bringing things with her. First she arrived with a table and chairs which she said she was taking to the Salvation Army until she realized I didn't have any. Then she carried in dishes and some sheets and pillowcases she didn't need. She even brought a large stereo with two wooden speakers that stood on the floor—and two men to hook it up. I watched as, little by little, she moved in.

We lived together for four long, difficult years. She was an alcoholic and manic-depressive, two disorders I knew nothing about. I stayed there and didn't know how to leave. I was beaten, stabbed, left out on lonely highways, and cursed repeatedly. All the people we knew thought she was a delight to be with. We had this terrible secret that she herself often forgot.

She was brutal when she beat me up time after time. She slept with a knife and cut me under my ear once while I was asleep. This made my face a little twisted. I woke up because of the taste of blood in my mouth. I asked her why she had done that and she laughed and said, "Let's make love. You're mine and I can do whatever I want with you. And if you won't be mine, you won't be anyone else's either." (Ana)

I hated being with her. I hated the way she treated me, the way she talked, the way she smelled. I hated her violence. But more than anything, I hated myself for not knowing how to leave. How could I ask anyone to help?

In the end, two things saved me. The first was an act of violence.

I'm a writer, so in times of desperation I frequently turn to words. Often, when Amy was drunk and would stand over me yelling or threatening to do the most terrible things, I'd take a notebook and pen and write. Anything. Whatever I thought of at the time. Sometimes I'd write down what she was saying instead of yelling back. I think she hated this. I wouldn't look at her, but would just grip the notebook and write. I had filled several notebooks this way.

And even though Judy said she was not afraid to die, I knew when they took her away that she was. I could see the fear in her eyes. They had so many chains and shackles on that poor woman—and she was frail and thin—that she couldn't walk and they had to wheelchair her out. Enough of that, I'm getting really sad. But I must say this, Judy died bravely and with dignity. (Andrea)

One day she grabbed my notebook and flung it away from me. She'd never done that before. I reacted immediately. Before I realized what I was doing, with a strength I didn't know I had, I grabbed her by the front of her blouse and slammed her up against the wall. Without loosening my grip I told her very slowly that if she ever did that again I would kill her. As I watched the blood drain from her face, I knew I had to get out.

A second saving grace was that a couple of weeks later I was hit by a car. The settlement that followed made leaving easier. When I had recovered sufficiently, I told Amy I was going to graduate school. Leaving my pain was much harder than I'd imagined. It had occupied a large place in my life. What would fill the hole?

I moved to Oklahoma, where this book begins.

Epilogue

It's seven in the morning when I open my curtains to look out at Pasture Fence Mountain. This is a mountain that has seen me through many seasons of my life, yet the mountain itself reflects little change.

Between my window and the piedmont there are two fields divided by a dirt road. Often, especially in the spring, a wall of rain starts at Skyline Drive and sweeps down the ridge with amazing fury. Without changing shape it crosses the first field, and when it hits the road, clouds of dust rise in the air. Many times, in awe at nature's force, I've rushed out to stand in the second field, the one closest to Amity, and waited for it to reach me, to wash over me and move on. I love that feeling of the rain pelting my skin, a ritual cleansing of sorts.

And I realize that this is why I've come back. This is Innisfree, and I've returned to write this book.

Several times during the past two months I've sent the manuscript to my editor and said it was finished. Just as many times she's returned to me and said it's not. She said it needs an ending, a final chapter, something that tells how I got to where I am today. I've consistently resisted this idea. But this morning, looking out at Pasture Fence Mountain and thinking about the rain, the cleansing part, that is, I realized that there is something I need to say.

For over twenty years I've deeply regretted what happened between Beth and me. I do not think now, nor did I think then, that it was right or good. And I do not want to give the impression by writing about it as I experienced it that I do not take full responsibility for what occurred. I accepted that responsibility years ago and went through many stages of self-loathing. Over time—and by time I mean years—I found a variety of ways, including abusive relationships, to punish myself for the fact that at one point in my life I allowed my needs override my common sense. After that I was afraid to let anyone close to me. Love, as I understood it, was out of the question.

Whenever I felt dangerously connected to anyone, I only had to remind myself that if this person really knew me, they would not want anything to do with me. For longer than I care to remember, the focus of my regret was that I had failed miserably as a human being. Perhaps only people who have started out to be perfect, as I did, can understand such a fall. But for myself there was no forgiveness.

Nine years ago, however, I saw the face of a God that recognized and loved the God-ness in me. I met a beautiful woman who loved me unconditionally. A woman who told me almost daily, and continues to tell me in so many ways, that being human is okay. That, as Sister Helen Prejean says, *I am better than my worst mistake.*

When this beloved woman, this dear friend, heard the terrible secret I'd carried with me for so many years, she only smiled and told me the legend of the cracked pot.

It's about this water bearer in India who had two large pots. Each hung on the end of a pole which she carried across her neck every day in order to collect water. One of the pots was perfect, as pots go, and always delivered a full portion of water from the stream to the main house. It was quite proud of its accomplishments. The other pot was cracked. So each day on the walk up the hill from the stream, the cracked pot lost much of the water, usually arriving half full at best. The pot was ashamed of its own imperfection and quite miserable that it could only manage to do half of what it was supposed to do. Several years passed, and it believed itself to be an abject failure.

One day the cracked pot spoke to the water bearer and said, "I am ashamed of myself and want to apologize to you."

"Why are you ashamed?" asked the water bearer.

"For two years I have only been able to deliver half of my load because this crack in my side causes the water to leak out. It is because of my flaws that you have so much extra work."

The water bearer felt great compassion for this pot and asked, "Did you notice that there are flowers on your side of the path where we walk each day?"

The pot admitted not noticing.

"They are only on your side," the water bearer explained. "That is because I have always known about your flaw and I took advantage of it. I planted seeds on your side of the path, and every day as we walk back from the stream you water them. For two years now, we have been able to enjoy great beauty because of who you are."

This woman who loves me told me we are all cracked pots and should not be afraid of our flaws. If we acknowledge them, they can be the cause of great beauty. In our weaknesses we may find our strength. For almost a decade she has loved me because I'm not perfect and because she found beauty in my flaws. Her unfaltering support has allowed me, in turn, to love and accept who I am. This is her greatest gift to me.

In the past few years, since I began writing about women on death row, I have been frequently asked, "How did you get this involved? How did you become so passionate about all this?" And up until writing this book I've always said, "It's because I met a woman on death row." Meaning, once I put a face to women on death row I could no longer ignore them. But now, after this, I might say, "It's because I saw my face on a woman on death row." I realized in my first interview with a woman awaiting execution that our similarities were quite substantial, our differences somewhat circumstantial.

Women on death row are recognized and known by their mistakes. I am both humbled and grieved that I have met so many women in these circumstances who have moved me to examine and change my own life. I can say without qualification that I know women on death row today who are much better human beings than I am. I am grateful that the circumstances in my life did not put me in the position they are in. But I see very clearly how that can happen.

The sun is setting on Pasture Fence Mountain. It has been a brilliant day, and there is a pink tint to the sky. I think of Jim, who checks with me each morning, saying, "Sky's blue?" and Matthew, who tells me in the afternoon, "Dark soon." This is Innisfree. I have written my book.

Firebrand Books is an award-winning feminist and lesbian publishing house. We are committed to producing quality work in a wide variety of genres by ethnically and racially diverse authors. Now in our fifteenth year, we have over one hundred titles in print.

A free catalog is available on request from Firebrand Books, 141 The Commons, Ithaca, New York 14850, 607-272-0000.

Visit our website at www.firebrandbooks.com.